ALL
THINGS
NEW

ALL THINGS NEW

Rethinking Sin, Salvation, and Everything in Between

FIONA *AND* TERRYL GIVENS

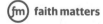

To request permissions, contact the publisher at info@faithmatters.org.

Hardcover: 978-1-953677-02-0
Paperback: 978-1-953677-00-6
Audiobook: 978-1-953677-01-3
Ebook: 978-1-953677-03-7

Library of Congress Number: 9781953677006

First edition October 2020.

Printed in the United States of America.

Faith Matters Publishing
2929 W Navigator Drive
Suite 400
Meridian, ID 83642

faithmatters.org

To our beloved grandchildren—

Sophie, Caleb, Georgia, Adelaide, Coraline, Lavinia, Alice, Laurelei, Emmy, Hazel, and the twins arriving soon, chased by their cousin and other grandchildren to follow

—who deserve a new vocabulary adequate to the broken world they will assist in healing.

Contents

Introduction

Evangelion (that we call the gospel) is a Greek word
and signifieth good, merry, glad and joyful tidings,
that maketh a man's heart glad, and maketh him
to sing, dance, and leap for joy.
—William Tyndale[1]

I f God weeps over our misery, why does Christ need to allay
God's wrath? If we are in a state of "awful woundedness," as
the angel tells Nephi, why do we call Christ our Savior rather
than our Healer?[2] If we are counseled, "Never shut the door of
your hearts to your children,"[3] why do we fear that our Father
will shut His? If Christ came "not to condemn the world," why
do we fear judgment? If Christ promises to "wipe away all tears,"
why do we anticipate untold sorrows to come in the next world?
If we are promised everything that we "are willing to receive,"
why are we filled with anxiety? We are told not to fear, but we
do. We are urged to rejoice, but we cannot. Something is wrong
with this picture.

Brigham Young said, "To profess to be a Saint, and not enjoy
the spirit of it, tries every fiber of the heart, and is one of the most
painful experiences that man can suffer."[4] Even as we partake of
the Plan of Happiness, the joy we should feel is impeded as we
continue along our fraught journey of life. Depression, poverty,
trauma, and illness, in ourselves and in those we love, are crosses
many bear. But one cross is needless and is borne by all too many
of us, and that one is the subject of this book.

A young woman wrote to us sharing her challenges as a missionary, wondering in moments of despair, "Why do I worship this God? . . . I couldn't sleep. Night after night I would lay in bed thinking about an angry, retributive God." We have heard these and similar sentiments expressed with great frequency. "I will wake up an hour or two before my alarm, only to have my mind flooded with thoughts of failings, sins, not fulfilling or magnifying a calling." From a grieving parent: "While waiting in the temple recently I came to [a scripture] about the damnation of those who fall from their covenants. I felt conflicted torment. What I read felt without hope. I begged God to understand." A man still hurting from "childhood wounds" described the belief that led him out of the Church: "It had always been a faith in an angry old-man-in-the-sky God. . . . The god I was raised to believe in was not kind, or loving, or merciful. Instead he was judgmental."

From another member, a letter expressed more heartache: "Over and over again, the connotations of the traditional language of the Gospel made me ache with fear and bitterness." Yet another recently wrote us about her journey toward healing: "Much of the depression I have experienced for years," she said with new self-understanding, "was because of Calvinist-type ideas that are in the Latter-day Saint culture." One student confessed, "I was the kind of child who heard, 'I am a Child of God' and instead of taking to heart the message of divine love, trembled at the second verse: 'Help me to understand his words before it grows too late.'" And another student described how "my understanding of the nature of God has evolved. . . . But as I've reflected on this, I've come to realize it isn't that I've learnt new things about God, rather that I have *unlearned* things about God—unhealthy, incorrect, culturally informed principles about God, which have in fact distanced me from God."

One question that came our way lingers with us still: "I often worry about how to navigate this fear with my future children in a culture where fear is, in a way, a starting point for obedience. What comes more naturally to a child—love or fear? Is it possible to teach your children to love you without them learning to fear you as a byproduct? Do these principles extend to our Heavenly Parents as well?" We believe that these and so many other struggling Saints are suffering as a consequence of what scripture calls "the traditions of the fathers, which [are] not correct" (Alma 21:17).

In 1 Nephi 13, the Lord's messenger characterizes the modern world's inhabitants as being in a state of "awful woundedness" (1830 edition) or in an "awful state of blindness" (1837 edition). And the specific, explicit reason given is the loss of the gospel's "plain and precious things." To what plain and precious things could the messenger be referring? Christians of past and present have believed in the Incarnation, the Atonement, and the Resurrection. If these are the most essential truths—and they are—then how can Christians of the past and Saints of the present be adrift in woundedness, blindness? The philosopher Friedrich Schleiermacher describes the situation well. He wrote that one can believe and teach that "everything is related to the redemption accomplished by Jesus of Nazareth" and yet that redemption can be "interpreted in such a way that it is reduced to incoherence."[5] His diagnosis is the subject of this book.

In some ways, we are still living and believing according to paradigms of the past. Describing the aftermath of those sixteenth-century revolutions in Christian thought launched by Luther and Calvin, a preeminent historian of religion writes, "The Reformation, particularly in its English Protestant form, has created the ideology dominant in the world's one remaining superpower, and Reformation and Counter-Reformation ways of thought remain (often alarmingly) alive and central in American culture."[6] For a Latter-day Saint, these survivals should be *especially* alarming, since we believe we have moved beyond them. Sadly, some have not. These "ways of thought" are part of an inheritance so vast, so ingrained, so pervasive that they reveal themselves in almost every thought, color every relationship, and can contaminate every religious conviction. "Behold, I make all things new," proclaimed the Lord (Rev. 21:5).[7] But many of us have missed the proclamation. We are still mired in the past, in ways we have not recognized.

The Doctrine and Covenants reinforces this continuing threat in the most alarming language. Joseph Smith referred to a "damning hand" that "riveted the creeds of the fathers, who have inherited lies, upon the hearts of the children, and filled the world with confusion." That confusion, he continued, "is now the very mainspring of all corruption, and the whole earth groans under the weight" (D&C 123:7). What can this mean, this reference to "the creeds of the fathers" that are riveted upon our hearts, filling us with confusion like "an iron yoke"?

To examine the inherited traditions that weigh us down and impede our joy in this world and our happiness in this Church is to provoke a more general topic: How are Saints to understand our relationship to other churches and to the Christian past in general? Our very identity as a people is inextricably connected with that Christian world against which we have defined ourselves and in light of which we stake our very claim to be members of a restored Church. To distill the pure essence of the gospel from the cultural trappings in which it can at times persist is a complex challenge for all of us. A better grasp of the Christian past can help us; so can familiarity with important theological developments. The place to begin would be with the foundations of the original Christianity, which the Saints claim has been restored. We may believe "in the same church" that existed anciently, but presumably the heart of the Restoration is more than offices and programs. What is the original core, the original meaning, of Christ's incarnation and teachings? *What,* in other words, was lost, and what most needed to be restored by Joseph Smith? Before the

Restoration, faith in Jesus Christ was widespread. The Word of God was in general circulation. Good Christians sought to love and serve their neighbors. What, then, was irretrievably broken? How, to put it in Schleiermacher's words, was the Original Story "reduced to incoherence"? Only when we answer those questions can we move on to recognize how our own vocabulary at times shares that "incoherence."

Chapter 1 offers a brief overview of what we might consider to be the essential nucleus of the original Christian message and the community that resulted. We will discuss two doctrines that were part of Christian self-understanding in the early years: the eternal nature of our souls, extending back beyond the formations of the world; and the parenthood of God taken as more than mere metaphor. These two sacred truths—the eternal nature of men and women, and the loving, selfless, devoted love of a parental God—were the lifeblood of a vibrant Christian community that saw the purpose of life as an educative experience in the school of love.

Chapter 2 consists of an extended foray into Christian history. Those without particular interest in historical details may wish to pass over this section; however, we would invoke the wisdom of James Baldwin, who in another context referred to "innocent people . . . trapped in a history which they do not understand and until they understand it, they cannot be released from it."[8] We believe that we cannot fully appreciate the destructive aspects of our inherited vocabulary unless we understand the sources of those cataclysmic—and catastrophic—changes that erased the doctrine of premortal life and reconfigured the nature of God. We focus our discussion on the two most formative moments of the Christian past: the late fourth century, dominated by the figure of Augustine, and the sixteenth century, which gave rise to the creeds so influential in Joseph Smith's day. Many beautiful and God-touched voices persisted through the centuries, and the motives of the religious figures who reconstructed the original gospel plan in new and detrimental ways were doubtless sincere and well-intentioned. Our purpose in rehearsing these developments is only in the interest of an improved understanding of how much further the Restoration must yet unfold to come fully "out of the wilderness" (D&C 5:14).

In chapter 3 we treat briefly those resources that both inform the work of Restoration and set its parameters: scripture and revelation. And, like the other crucial vocabulary this book reexamines, *scripture* and *revelation* are also words that we might with profit reconsider. With these preparatory chapters establishing the groundwork, the chapters that follow constitute the bulk and primary object of our study: our suggestions for how—in the light of Restoration understanding—we might move ahead the project of constituting a religious vocabulary more fitting to a dispensation in which all things are new.

NOTES

1   David Daniell, *William Tyndale: A Biography* (New Haven, CT: Yale University Press, 1994), 123.

2   1 Nephi 13:32, 1830 edition. The 1837 and present editions replace "state of awful woundedness" with "awful state of blindness." The common point of both descriptive words is telling: woundedness and blindness alike describe a condition for which we are not responsible; the injury is due to the agency of others who have removed "plain and precious" things from the scriptural record.

3   Robert D. Hales, North America Northeast Area broadcast (April 26, 2015).

4   Brigham Young, *Complete Discourses*, ed. Richard S. Van Wagoner (Salt Lake City: Smith-Pettit Foundation, 2009), 5:2540.

5   Quoted in Alister McGrath, *Heresy: A History of Defending the Truth* (New York: HarperOne, 2009), 93.

6   Diarmaid MacCulloch, *The Reformation: A History* (New York: Viking, 2004), xxii.

7   Unless otherwise indicated, biblical citations are from the King James Version.

8   James Baldwin, "My Dungeon Shook: Letter to My Nephew on the One Hundredth Anniversary of the Emancipation," in *The Fire Next Time* (New York: Dial Press, 1963), 21. Cited in Joanna Brooks, *Mormonism and White Supremacy* (New York: Oxford University Press, 2020), 85–86.

PART ONE

Foundations

CHAPTER ONE

The First Christians

Radical Love and Community

I (Terryl) grew up in Lynchburg, Virginia, a town at that time dominated by fervent evangelicals. My brother and I, at school and on the street, were frequently approached by young people asking us, "Have you been saved?" I was just inclining toward religion (as a baptized but long inactive Latter-day Saint), but the question had absolutely no traction with me. First, I didn't feel in danger of damnation; second, I had no idea what evangelicals' conception of damnation really meant; and third, it didn't seem that any condition worth aspiring to could be attained by on-the-spot verbal confession—even if sincere. As I analyze such encounters now, decades later, my question is, How did Christians move from the man and message depicted in the New Testament to these zealous missionaries offering to save me from damnation? Is there a readily discernible core to that world-changing revolution of two thousand years ago? And if so, in what key ways was that essential core transformed—and deformed—in succeeding centuries?

David Bentley Hart characterizes the mortal Incarnation of Jesus Christ, what Nephi calls the "condescension of God," this way: "History has been invaded by God in Christ in such a way that nothing can stay as it was. All terms of human community and conduct have been altered at the deepest levels."[1] But altered how, precisely? What changed with the advent of Christ and His teachings? Why, having encountered Him, could we no longer "be at ease here," in T. S. Eliot's words, "with an alien people clutching their gods?"[2] For Hart, what changed were the "terms of human community and conduct." By itself, that reason seems to be severely inadequate. *Why* did Christianity represent a revised imperative to build community and act according to new norms? Many religious revolutionaries from Buddha to Gandhi have instigated new codes of conduct and ideals for community-building. Did Jesus preach something yet more radical?

A partial answer is implicit in Hart's earlier phrase: something about the *way* in which God "invaded" history "in Christ." For Hart—and most Christians—Christ represents a unique instance of God being made visible and approachable to us. We can now "walk through the fog of God toward the clarity of Christ," in one poet's words.[3] This accessibility to God is generally called the miracle of the "Incarnation." God, the invisible, the incomprehensible, the Creator of the Universe, "wrapt in night's mantle, stole into a manger."[4]

The Christian church would spend the next four centuries struggling to work out the precise meaning of that Incarnation, that "such a way" of God becoming Christ. Church councils and church fathers were so preoccupied with that question that they seemed to have mental effort for little else. At Nicaea and Chalcedon, in chambers and treatises, they debated: Was Christ distinct from the Father? A mode or aspect of the Father? Of similar substance to the Father? Of the same substance as the Father? Subordinate to the Father? Fully equal? Coeternal with the Father? Begotten? Made?

Those questions are largely academic, and today they mostly fail to interest, motivate, or inspire us. Can we back up and ask the question again? *Before the theologians took over the conversation*, what was it about *Christ*—the person and the message—that was galvanizing, transformative, and so appealing that it led a small band of Galileans to reshape the world and lay the foundations for a church of billions? That seems a more fruitful direction of inquiry. Let's go back to the beginning and reassess in what the original Christian revolution consisted.

One possibility: In Christ, for the first and only time in human history, we see ourselves as we are meant to become. We see in Christ our own possible destiny: to be fully and completely like Him. Infinite love and goodness have a form, a face, a healing hand—that reaches out to touch, to embrace. This, we discover to our shock and surprise, this is God. For Christ, we learn, is not a mere earthly version of a distant, unapproachable, "foggy" God. God the Son is the perfect reflection of exactly who God the Father always was and is: "He that hath seen me hath seen the Father" (John 14:9). This is not a metaphor, not mystic wisdom, but the plain and precious truth unveiled. So when God the Son says, to our even greater shock and surprise, "Come, follow me," He is saying much more than modern Christians realize. Joseph Smith merely restated the astounding essence of Christ's original message: "God found Himself in the midst of spirits and glory." And "He saw proper to institute laws whereby the rest, who were less in intelligence, could have a privilege to advance like Himself and be exalted with Him."[5] To follow Christ *is* to follow His footsteps in becoming what He is: a "joint-heir" of God, as Paul called us (Rom. 8:17).

John, the most intimate of Christ's disciples and friends, and perhaps the most reliable of His chroniclers, understood history's invasion by God in just such terms. In his first epistle, he expresses with poignant simplicity the essence of the Good News: "See what love the Father has given us, that we should be called the children of God; and that is what we are. The reason the world does not know us is that it did not know him. Beloved, we are God's children now; what we will be has not yet been revealed. What we do

know is this: when he is revealed, we will be like him." (1 John
3:2 [New Rev. Standard Version]). The original message was one
of appalling wonder and sublime simplicity: "[Jesus] declares to
His Father, in language not to be easily mistaken, that he wanted
His disciples, even all of them, to be as himself and the Father."[6]
And that never-varying ambition extends to every member of
every nation, kindred, and tongue, who will come and "partake
of the waters of life freely" (D&C 10:66).

We may have a hard time feeling the shock of that astonishing idea: God walks among us as a minister and mentor and
fellow traveler. He breaks bread with His friends, weeps over the
death of a friend, dines with sinners, and washes the feet of His
apostles. God the Son then tells us that we, daughters and sons,
may be "glorified together" with Him (Rom. 8:17).

It was this same John, according to tradition, who heard the
Lord proclaim, "See, I am making all things new" (Rev. 21:5). *All*
things. A new identity foreshadows a new destiny. We who saw
ourselves only "in a mirror, dimly" (1 Cor. 13:12) are suddenly
God's progeny, in preparation to be coheirs with Christ. If the
literal *imitatio Dei* (imitation of God) is the first great principle,
then the second principle now emerges. A universal Parent meant
a universal sisterhood and brotherhood among all people.

The idea took concrete, transformative shape. According
to the early church father Tertullian (ca. 160–240 AD), the first
Christians were ridiculed "because we call each other brother
and sister." This was no mere metaphor; their understanding of
the interrelatedness of the human family as a whole was utterly
transformative of every connection, every gesture, every aspiration
toward genuine community. For as these early Christians insisted
to a skeptical world, "We are your brothers and sisters as well."
New paradigms bring forth new fruits. "What marks us in the eye
of our enemies is our practice of lovingkindness: 'Only look,' they
say, 'how they love one another.'"[7] These first Christians turned

ad hoc communities into a society governed by love. A historian of early Christianity confirms the world-defying novelty and its results: the catalyst to the Christian revolution was "the presence of a group joined by Spiritual power into an extended family."[8]

How novel was the concept of a universal love—a love that encompasses the entire human family within God's embrace—and eventually in our embrace as well? The Jewish scholar Meir Soloveichik asserts that this concept did not spring from Christianity's antecedents. "To my knowledge not a single Jewish source asserts that God deeply desires to save all humanity, nor that he loves every member of the human race," he writes.[9] The way in which early Christians understood—and practiced—love was a marvel to all who witnessed it, their detractors and disciples alike. The fourth-century monk Rufinus described how Christians treated strangers:

> Then we came to Nitria, the best-known of all the monasteries of Egypt, about forty miles from Alexandria. . . . As we drew near to that place and they realized that foreign brethren were arriving, they poured out of their cells like a swarm of bees and ran to meet us with delight and alacrity, many of them carrying containers of water and of bread. . . . When they had welcomed us, first of all they led us with psalms into the church and washed our feet and one by one they dried them with the linen cloth they were girded with, as if to wash away the fatigue of the journey. . . . What can I say that would do justice to their humanity, their courtesy, and their love? Nowhere have I seen love flourish so greatly, nowhere with such quick compassion, such eager hospitality.[10]

Christian love transcended anything the ancient world had seen. Rodney Stark notes how through recurrent plagues, as citizens fled infected areas, Christians remained behind to nurse and minister to the sick at the cost of their lives. Around 260 AD, at the height of yet another epidemic, the Christian Dionysius recorded,

> Christians showed unbounded love and loyalty, never sparing themselves and thinking only of one another. Heedless of danger, they took charge of the sick, attending to their every need and ministering to them in Christ, and with them departed this life serenely happy; for they were infected by others with the disease, drawing on themselves the sickness of their neighbors and cheerfully accepting their pains. Many, in nursing and curing others, transferred their death to themselves and died in their stead.[11]

In exploring the appeal of early Christianity, the cynic Friedrich Nietzsche could only marvel at the gullibility of the teeming throngs of converts who had found this "better way." Power and dominion were the source of the only real happiness, he insisted. The rich, the well-born, the noble—these possessed the genuine article, until clever priests convinced them that some phantom joy was only found in pity, humility, selflessness and fellow-feeling. (A "slave-revolt in morality" he called it.)[12] Yet even that great skeptic could not explain how the noble, the powerful, the rich—how they too were persuaded to willingly forsake their privilege and aspire instead to humility, to selflessness, to compassion.

Christianity survived amid pogroms and persecutions (and suspicious philosophers) because it quenched a thirst that had never found perfect resolution: as Martin Buber diagnosed the essential human condition, "The longing for relation is primary, the cupped hand into which the being that confronts us nestles."[13] Christianity revealed the Spirit's true lineaments hidden beneath the world of transactional relationships based on commerce, power dynamics, and self-interest. Christianity exposed the deeper roots of our being: fragmented individuals finding fulness only in a thriving web of relationships. And pervading these relationships was a principle unseen in human history: the dissolution of hierarchy, status, and oppressive power dynamics; full equality in Christ. One historian notes, "The lasting impression left by the early Church membership is one of social diversity. Yet it went with an ideal of human equality: in Christ, taught the Christians, all were equal, and the distinctions of rank and degree were irrelevant. In church meetings, educated people sat as equals among other men's slaves and petty artisans."[14]

The revolution never found its perfect form, but the template for Zion had been drawn: "Here there is no Gentile or Jew, circumcised or free" (Col. 3:11). Nor, said Paul, "is there male and female." For "in the Lord woman is not independent of man or man independent of woman" (Gal. 3:28; 1 Cor. 11:11). "The Magna Carta of Humanity," one scholar called this Pauline pronouncement. "There is nothing like it in all of antiquity."[15] The very angels of this new dispensation call themselves our "fellowservants" (Rev. 22:9). And had not even Christ, King of kings, washed the feet of His disciples and said, "I do not call you servants . . . but I have called you friends" (John 15:15)? Diversity but not division; variety but equality.

God's love is going to be a central theme in what follows, so clarity is essential here. Love has been so commodified, trivialized, and banalized that it is hard to break free of cliché in describing love's new dominion over human connectedness that the Christian message ushered in. And yet, as with the Zion of the Nephites, love's dominion was short-lived. This is immediately evident to the most casual student of Christian history, which is essentially one long chronicle of the unspeakable brutality of man against man. How was a gospel rooted and grounded in love employed to justify genocide, crusades, pogroms, torture? How did we travel from the revolutionary circles of compassion for which Christianity was known, to the Inquisition and wars of religious persecution? Another way of framing this question is, Can we in fact find the root of Christianity's grievous wounds—and thereby trace the need for the Restoration—in the distortion and corruption of the meaning of Divine Love and in the forms it took in the institutional church?

Clearly, at some point in the Christian past, God's love was horribly debased, and believers' understanding of it was warped and perverted. We find a powerful instance of, and explanation for, this progressive corruption of love in reading Dante's *Inferno*, a long poem that describes a pilgrim's journey through the circles of hell, escorted by his guide, the poet Virgil. Though rightly heralded as a masterwork of Western civilization, we find in this medieval work a deeply distorted and disturbing sense of God and God's love. At one point, Dante sees the agony of a tortured soul and asks the reader, "how I could check my tears, when near at hand / I saw the image of our humanity distorted so. . . . Certainly I wept." Seeing Dante's compassion, Virgil rounds on Dante furiously: "Still? Still like the other fools? There is no place / for pity here. Who is more arrogant / within his soul, who is more impious / than one who dares to sorrow at God's judgment?"[16]

In a different scene, Dante sees another sinner trying to find respite from his sufferings by latching on to the boat he and Virgil are traveling in. This time, Dante responds differently: "May you weep and wail to all eternity, for I know you, hell-dog, filthy as you are." He beats the sinner off, with his guide shouting "Down! Down! With the other dogs!" Then Virgil turns to Dante and embraces him, saying: "Indignant spirit, I kiss you as you frown. Blessed be she who bore you."[17]

We find the contrast between Dante's naturally compassionate, tender-hearted response and that of a hardened and judgmental tormentor horrifying—and instructive. The transition in Dante is horrifying because of the sheer spectacle of rationalized brutality. And it is horrifyingly instructive because we see in his transition an almost casual instance of the implicit argument that *God's* love is of an entirely different complexion than *our* love—that it is not just quantitatively superior to ours but qualitatively distinct and foreign to our innate compassion. By attributing such "love" to a God who in those early centuries was coming to be situated beyond human categories of comprehension, one could reshape it in any deformed way one chose and call it "love." Now we begin to understand how, starting a few centuries before the medieval period, Christians were routinely burning men and women alive and massacring other humans by the thousands in the name of God's love.[18] "Their bodies must be destroyed that their souls may be saved," wrote one papal legate.[19]

Here is how one Christian celebrated the fruits of the First Crusade (1066–99): "If you had been there you would have seen our feet colored to our ankles with the blood of the slain. But what more shall I relate? None of them [the Muslims] were left alive; neither women nor children were spared. Afterward, all clergy, laymen went to the Sepulcher of the Lord and His glorious temple singing. With fitting humility, they repeated prayers and made their offering at the holy places they had long desired to visit."[20]

Our point is not that Christians have committed atrocities in God's name while preaching He is a God of love. That is true, but it is also a tired cliché. Our point is that the way we imagine God's love had to undergo a process of contamination and dreadful distortion before Christians could readily believe, as Dante did, that a God of love rejoiced in the screams and blood of His children. This particular transformation is powerful evidence of why theology is not just abstract speculation disconnected from the demands of real life in the world. Francine Bennion has asked, "Does [theology] really matter . . . ? Can't we just be kind and patient, without worrying about various points of theology?

It matters," she insists.[21] And it does. Even a word as universally recognized as *love* has radically different forms, manifestations, and effectual meanings, depending on the framework of belief in which we use it. History proves that moral mayhem may result when "the distinctively Christian love" is "cut loose from its theological moorings."[22] This, in fact, is a principal thesis of this book. As one example, a historian described the medieval consequences of the transformations of *love* we are here illustrating: "The truest kindness was cruelty; the truest mercy harshness."[23] How and when did that shift occur? How did we arrive, for the majority of Christian history, at a God who—in the words of one hugely influential medieval voice—"looks upon us in our wretchedness . . . [but] feels not the effect. . . . Saves the wretched, . . . [but] is touched by no fellow-suffering in that wretchedness"?[24]

Edward Beecher (1803–95) spoke truly when he warned that "of all errors, none are so fundamental and so wide reaching in their evil tendencies and results as errors with respect to the character of God."[25] We should all be alarmed—concerned at least—to realize how susceptible we are, as products of our own historical inheritance, to having our view of God shaped by cultural conditioning. Belonging to the restored Church does not make us immune to such influences. Remember that Joseph Smith was speaking to Latter-day Saints when he warned of the tenacity of inherited traditions, calling them "handcuffs, and chains, and shackles." But he also suggested optimism about the way forward: "A *correct* idea of His character, perfections and attributes," he taught, was essential to a transformative faith.[26] For Joseph Smith, an absolutely fundamental purpose of the Restoration was to replace the slanderous character imputed to God with a *correct* understanding consistent with the original Good News.

Clearly, Christians have recently made great strides in returning to holier and more wholesome conceptions of God. Rob Bell has taught millions about a God who intends to save the entire human family. N. T. Wright has worked to shift the heart of Christian concern from personal salvation to societal justice, Timothy Keller emphasizes the prodigality of God's love, and Richard Rohr advocates a more gentle, contemplative, and hopeful Christian practice. On many fronts, Christianity is experiencing renewal and revitalization. Latter-day Saints can find much to applaud and much to learn from earnest God- and Truth-seekers across the spectrum. Other religions of the world similarly have much to teach us about lives of compassion and holiness. At the same time, Latter-day Saints have a battery of resources available to us that we have not fully explored in our quest for a religion that is "pure and undefiled" (James 1:27).

In particular, we have an outline of the Great Story, the Original Plan, that provides us a more ample context, as well as additional compass points, to orient ourselves and make sense of the journey. This background can fully rectify the damage done by the long chain of historical assaults on God's character. Recuperating this Great Story gives context to the kind of absolute love we ascribe to God. It reveals the primeval setting in which that love launched the plan of human happiness, and the story gives concrete embodiment and recognizable form to the love that undergirds the universe and our place within it.

The Great Story has two pivotal features. When these two features disappeared, the whole Christian vocabulary became unmoored from its foundations, and meanings become fractured, disjointed, recast. *Salvation, heaven, the Fall, sin, repentance, forgiveness, justice, atonement, grace, obedience, worthiness,* and *judgment* all have come to mean something very different from what they meant in the context of a different story, with a different beginning and a different plot. The two pivotal features of the Great Story are (1) the premortality of humans and (2) the parenthood of God. We believe that inherent in these two seminal concepts are the seeds of the only gospel understanding that can fully address what

Nephi called "the state of awful woundedness" that we inhabit. Thinking through the implications of those two ideas can help us excise from our language the destructive "traditions of the fathers" that, in Joseph Smith's language, have filled the world—and sometimes the minds of the Saints—"with confusion." So let us look at how those two ideas ground an entire gospel framework; then we will turn to examine the catastrophe that ensued when those ideas were exiled from Christian history.

Premortality

Premortality is *not* just an addendum to the story of human life. If you change the beginning, you change the ending—and everything in between. Our story begins with freely acting, independent, divine spirits who are presented with an invitation—eons before planet earth exists. Beings of perfect holiness proposed giving an innumerable host of intelligences in whose midst They dwelt a pathway to Their own exalted condition. For those willing to endure a "discipline [education] of suffering,"[27] full participation in an exalted Heavenly Family was promised. If you live in this world, then you were one of those who chose to engage in "the trial by existence," in the poet's words, while those who lingered behind "view once more the sacrifice of those who, for some good discerned, will gladly give up paradise."[28] We chose this existence because of an "everlasting covenant" into which we entered, receiving our Parents' assurance that Their "work and glory" was to bring about our "immortality and eternal life" (Moses 1:39). "*Their* goal, *their* work, and *their* glory," taught Theodore M. Burton (our emphasis).[29] In Brigham Young's economical summary of the opening curtain in the human saga, our "divine spirit," he said, would be joined to a body. Then this body and spirit work jointly toward sanctification, until that day comes when "we may love all with a divine affection."[30] Our first apostolic theologian,

Parley Pratt, elaborated: "Our natural affections . . . are the very mainsprings of life and happiness—they are the cement of all virtuous and heavenly society. . . . Aided and directed by the light of heaven . . . every affection, attribute, power and energy of your body and mind may be cultivated, increased, enlarged, perfected . . . for the glory and happiness of yourself, and all of those whose good fortune it may be to be associated with you."[31]

We have heard this story countless times, but its ramifications never sound worn to the perceptive listener. Our lives and destiny are grounded in the confidence of divine beings—in Their confidence that They can shepherd us, gods in embryo, to be the kind of beings, in the kind of relationships, that constitute life eternal. A love beyond imagining prompted the proposal, and a love of infinite potency will assure the proposal's consummation. We may wander, stumble, or lose our bearings, but the promise "thou art ever with me, and all that I have is thine" was engraved in our hearts (Luke 15:31). God "ever keepeth us in His blessed love."[32]

The Restoration clarification of our beings as eternal rather than created is a seismic theological shift. In the Book of Abraham, humanity is referred to as "intelligences," "spirits," and "souls." The names are used interchangeably, denoting a core of human identity without beginning or end. As Aristotle stated, "That which is created cannot be free,"[33] which means that agency could not exist, let alone flourish, if we were created beings. (The creator is responsible for the nature [and failures] of the created, whether cookies, a bridge, or a human soul.) While our theology does not put us on a par with God originally, it does make clear that we are consubstantial with God, in that we are, essentially, divine, eternal beings. And our theology makes us not willing subjects of the Father's plan but collaborators in its very inception. A close reading of Abraham 3:22–24 suggests that premortal spirits were engaged in the organization of the world. "And there stood one among them [spirits/souls/intelligences] that was like unto God, and he said unto those who were with him: We will go down, for there is space there, and we will take of these materials, and we will make an earth whereon these may dwell."

These backgrounds to our premortal life, mortality's purpose, and divine vocation were fairly widespread in the first few centuries of the church. We see this teaching in the New Testament (John 9) and in the writings of church fathers and theologians whose names are now unfamiliar to the average Latter-day Saint: Pseudo-Clement, Clement of Alexandria, Origen, Evagrius, Didymus the Blind, Synesius of Cyrene, Nemesius, Cyril of Jerusalem, Jerome, and the most influential church father of them all—the young Augustine. In the words of Origen, the doctrine's foremost expositor and defender, "You (the soul) could not have reached the palm-groves unless you had experienced the harsh trials; you could not have reached the gentle springs without first having to overcome sadness and difficulties. . . . The education of the soul is an age-long spiritual adventure." It began in premortal realms, "continuing after death."[34] With this truth in mind, as we hope to show, it is impossible to understand *salvation, heaven, the fall, sin, judgment*, or kindred terms in the ways that our brothers and sisters in other Christian traditions do.

Parenthood of God

William Ellery Channing called "the parental character of God" "the first great doctrine of Christianity."[35] However, this doctrine is meaningful and efficacious only to the extent that it is read as more than sentimental analogy or impoverished metaphor. Parents who understand their sacred role love in a particular way, with particular selflessness and steadfastness. They seek the good of their children above their own. They give direction and counsel, exercise forgiveness, know and feel and understand—all in ways vastly different than is the case with kings and sovereigns on the one hand and unfeeling and unmovable Platonic entities on the other. Parental love is absolute, it is redemptive, it is universal, and it is unshakable. As with our understanding of our origin in those premortal realms, an inspired understanding of God as our actual Father and Mother before creation's dawn is radically incompatible with centuries of Christian writings about human nature, the Fall, Atonement, repentance, forgiveness, worthiness, justice, or kindred terms in our religious language.

Parents, of course, comprise a companionship. That a Heavenly Father is joined in eternal partnership with a Heavenly Mother is no small contribution to current religious understanding. Heavenly Mother's emergence out of obscurity changes everything. Profoundly. This doctrine, and this doctrine alone, not only (1) for the first time in modern human history, fully dignifies one half of the human race but also (2) makes possible and reasonable a return to an anthropomorphic God, a God in whose image we all are. In addition, the doctrine of Heavenly Mother (3) lays the groundwork for a truly sociable heaven, in which the relationships of family association flourish, and (4) suggests that a change in pronoun usage may be in order. In the paragraphs that follow, we will discuss each of these four points in more detail.

(1) In the Christian West, as the great feminist figure Elizabeth Cady Stanton recognized, any challenge to patriarchal supremacy, any movement in the direction of equality between the sexes, could emerge only in defiance of, or in blatant disregard for, traditional Christian dogma. This is because Christianity posited a male supreme deity who existed in gendered isolation. And it made any ideal of god-like striving predicated on a male model. Stanton wrote, "The first step in the elevation of woman to her true position, as an equal factor in human progress, is the cultivation of the religious sentiment in regard to her dignity and equality, the recognition by the rising generation of an ideal Heavenly Mother."[36] She could not find specific biblical basis for

her reconstruction of the Trinity but thought the "let *us*" of Genesis opened a door. Since her time, an abundant and flourishing scholarship has found numerous traces of the Feminine Divine in the biblical text, as well as in a host of extra-biblical and archaeological sources.[37] The Latter-day Saint reconstruction of Eve's role as noble pioneer rather than frail defaulter accomplished much work toward assigning to woman a place of equal privilege and honor. Recuperating our Heavenly Mother was even more momentous. For it makes the ideal of exaltation, of the *imitatio Dei*, the full and complete imitation of the divine, a living possibility, a vivid option for both woman and man alike.

The existence of a Mother in Heaven is more than a theological proposition. It can be a transformative reality. The apostle Erastus Snow taught that "to [the Saints] this great truth is most precious, precious to contemplate, and it is an inexpressible privilege to be able to draw nigh unto Him and say 'Our Father' . . . And immediately this great truth is impressed upon our minds, we very naturally begin to associate it with the idea of mother."[38]

(2) When Joseph reworked the Genesis account of creation, he made this significant revision: "In the day that God created man, in the likeness of God made he him; *in the image of His own body*, male and female, created He them" (Moses 6:9; our emphasis). That revision may be the earliest hint of Joseph's awareness that the Father comprised one-half of the category "God." In addition to a He there has to be a She if both Adam *and* Eve are in God's *bodily* image. If God does have a body, then it would have to be the template for the entire human family. This is made even clearer in Joseph's production of the Book of Abraham: "The *Gods* went down to organize man in *their* own image, in the image of the Gods to form they him, *male and female* to form they them" (Abr. 4:27; note here that Joseph has recast the word *create* as *organize*, recognizing the eternity of our intelligence, or essential identity).

(3) What we know of love we first learn from our place in a web of relationships. Eternal life, which we understand to be the kind of life God leads, incorporates not just Their character, but the relationality that defines Their existence and is the source of Their joy. Life as a school of love finds greater meaning and relevance if we anticipate that the bonds we form, our connections and attachments and shared intimacy, are not transient but are preparations for an eternal sociability modeled on this one. We learn to "love all with a divine affection," as Brigham Young said.

(4) Elder John A. Widtsoe wrote: "The glorious vision of life hereafter . . . is given radiant warmth by the thought that . . . [we have] a mother who possesses the attributes of Godhood."[39] The Apostle Erastus Snow went further: "Deity consists of man and woman. . . . I have another description: There never was a God, and there never will be in all eternities, except they are made of these two component parts; a man and a woman; the male and the female."[40] If this is true, then when we employ the term *God*, it will often be the case that two divine Beings are behind the expression. The writer of Genesis employed the name Adam to refer to a fully collaborative couple; *Adam* is effectively their surname (Gen. 5:2; Moses 6:9). Just as Adam can refer to both Adam and Eve, there will there be instances when *God* is rightly followed by the pronoun *They*.[41] Brigham Young taught that "we were created . . . in the image of our father and our mother, the image of our God." His statement indicates that calling Heavenly Mother "God" is consistent with the biblical account of the creation of both the "male and female" being in "the image of God" (Gen. 1:26–27).

These two doctrines—our premortal life with the plans there set in motion and the true parental nature of God—are the foundations of the Restoration and are unique in the current Christian world. Their significance is the reason why a wholesale

rehabilitation of religious vocabulary is called for. To quote
Edward Beecher once more, "If there is in fact a malignant
spirit, of great and all-pervading power, intent on making a
fixed and steady opposition to the progress of the cause of God,"
he would "pervert and disgrace" the story of our true origins
in a premortal world, and our true relation to God. We now
turn to a discussion of how those two truths were lost and with
what catastrophic—and lingering—results.

NOTES

1   David Bentley Hart, *The New Testament: A Translation* (New Haven: Yale University Press, 2017), xxiii–xxiv.

2   T. S. Eliot, "Journey of the Magi," in *The Compete Poems and Plays 1909–1950* (New York: Harcourt, Brace, and World, 1971), 69.

3   Christian Wiman, *My Bright Abyss* (New York: Farrar, Straus and Giroux, 2014), 121.

4   George Herbert, "Christmas," in *The Complete English Works* (New York: Knopf, 1995), 78.

5   Stan Larson, "The King Follett Discourse: A Newly Amalgamated Text," *BYU Studies* 18, no. 2 (Winter 1978): 204.

6   Theology Lecture Seventh, 1835 D&C, p. 69. (These writings are now known as the *Lectures on Faith*).

7   Elaine Pagels, *Beyond Belief: The Secret Gospel of Thomas* (New York: Random House, 2003), 10.

8   Pagels, *Beyond Belief*, 6.

9   Meir Soloveichik, "The Virtue of Hate," *First Things* 130 (2003): 43–44.

10   Diana Butler Bass, *A People's History of Christianity* (New York: HarperCollins, 1989), 64.

11   Quoted in Rodney Stark, *The Rise of Christianity* (New York: HarperCollins, 1996), 82.

12   Friedrich Nietzsche makes this argument in his *Genealogy of Morals* (1887).

13   Martin Buber, *I and Thou*, trans. Walter Kaufmann (New York: Touchstone, 1996), 78.

14   Robin Lane Fox, *Pagans and Christians* (New York: Knopf, 1987), 337.

15   John J. Collins, *What Are Biblical Values: What the Bible Says on Key Ethical Issues* (New Haven: Yale University Press, 2019), 137.

16   Dante, *Inferno*, trans. John Ciardi (New York: Mentor, 1982), canto 20, lines 21–30, p. 175.

17   Dante, *Inferno*, canto 8, lines 37–43, p. 81.

18   "Even when persons were burned at the stake, the prevailing belief was that such burning would free their souls for redemption." Robert D. Hanser, *A Brief Introduction to Corrections* (Thousand Oaks, CA: Sage, 2021), 5. A papal bull declared that such punishment was in accord with "the will of the Spirit" (Exsurge Domine, 15 June 1520).

19   These words were those of Cardinal Girolamo Aleander. The Protestants, for their part, made the same arguments and justifications in the opposite direction. "Germans should wash their hands in the blood of papists," according to Luther. Quoted in Michael Massing, *Fatal Discord: Erasmus, Luther, and the Fight for the Western Mind* (New York: HarperCollins, 2018), 448–49.

20   Bass, *People's History*, 134.

21   Francine R. Bennion, "A Latter-day Saint Theology of Suffering," in *At the Pulpit*, ed. Jennifer Reeder and Kate Holbrook (Salt Lake City: Church Historian's Press, 2017), 220.

22   Tom Holland, *Dominion: How the Christian Revolution Remade the World* (New York: Basic Books, 2019), 493. Holland, in those words, has in mind the transformed landscape of the American 1960s.

23   Holland, *Dominion*, 254.

24   The words are from Anselm (1033–1109), *Proslogion* 8, quoted in in Nicholas Wolterstorff, "Suffering Love," in *Augustine's Confessions: Critical Essays*, ed. William E. Mann, (London: Rowman and Littlefield, 2006), 120; spelling modernized.

25   Edward Beecher, *The Concord of Ages* (New York: Derby & Jackson, 1860), 156.

26   Theology Lecture Third, 1835 D&C p. 36.

27   Beecher, *Concord*, 98.

28   Robert Frost, "Trial by Existence," in *Poetry of Robert Frost*, ed. Edward Connery Lathem (New York: Hold, Rinehard, and Winston, 1969), 20.

29   Theodore M. Burton, "A Marriage to Last Through Eternity," *Ensign* 17, no. 6 (June 1987): 12–15.

30   Richard S. Van Wagoner, ed., *The Complete Discourses of Brigham Young* (Salt Lake City: Smith-Petit Foundation, 2009), 3:1897.

31   Parley P. Pratt, *An Appeal to the Inhabitants of the State of New York; Letter to Queen Victoria; The Fountain of Knowledge; Immortality of the Body; and Intelligence and Affection* (Nauvoo, IL: John Taylor, [1844]).

32   Denise N. Baker, ed., *The Showings of Julian of Norwich*, 1.5 (New York: Norton, 2005), 10.

33   Aristotle, *Metaphysics*, 1.2.

34   Origen, *Homilies on Numbers* 27.11, in *Doctrine of the Soul in the Thought of Plotinus and Origen*, by Antonia Tripolitis (Roslyn Heights, NY: Libra, 1977), 126; and *De Principiis* 2.11.6–7, paraphrased in Tripolitis, *Doctrine of the Soul*, 133.

35   William Ellery Channing, "The Essence of the Christian Religion," in *Works* (Boston: American Unitarian Association, 1899), 1004. Quoted by Jeffrey Holland in "A Perfect Brightness of Hope," *Ensign* 50, no. 5 (May 2020): 81.

36   Elizabeth Cady Stanton, *The Woman's Bible* (New York: Prometheus Books, 1999), 14.

37   For a survey that places developments in the context of the Latter-day Saint tradition, see Fiona Givens, "Feminism and Heavenly Mother," in *Encyclopedia of Mormon Gender and Feminism* (New York: Routledge, 2020).

38   Erastus Snow, "Discourse by Apostle Erastus Snow," *Deseret News*, October 22, 1884, 2.

39   John A. Widtsoe, "Everlasting Motherhood," *Millennial Star* 90 (May 10, 1928).

40   Erastus Snow, in *Journal of Discourses*, 19:266.

41   Obviously, we can't presume to discern all those instances in which *God* might be taken to refer to Heavenly Father and Heavenly Mother as an exalted couple in Erastus Snow's sense. However, we will use the pronoun *They* when context suggests to us that the term can apply to both with clear validity.

CHAPTER TWO

Double Catastrophe
Augustine and the Reformation

Creeds

The invasion of history by Christ originally reconfigured our whole conceptual universe: the kind of being we are, who our God is, Their aspirations for us, and how we negotiate the perilous path back to Their presence. What we believe about these vital subjects has incalculable influence on how we love, and how we live. Jesus ministered and taught for three short years, in a remote corner of the Middle East, to a small audience of the largely marginalized, dispossessed, and wounded. His recorded words are numbered in the mere hundreds and are more concerned with moral instruction and healing encounters than doctrinal content. So, what constitutes the body of early Christian teachings is extrapolation; it is the fruit of improvisation, elaboration, and, to a debatable extent, inspiration. It is not surprising that before the New Testament is even canonized we find varying schools of thought, competing orthodoxies, schisms, and heresies. Regrettably, the cumulative effect over succeeding generations is to rewrite the core narrative in tragically destructive ways.

God-touched souls have recurrently provided pinpricks of light amid the greater darkness. We agree with the historian of religion Diana Bass, who writes that "the [Christian] church has never gotten it completely right. But it has not gotten it completely wrong either."[1] Our point is that when the dominant institutions *did* "get it wrong," they often got it tragically, horrendously, catastrophically wrong. If that sounds like hyperbole, history says otherwise. The first decisive turning points came with a collision of ideas and personalities in the fourth century. Out of the ashes of that conflict emerged the Christianity that would dominate the world for the next eleven hundred years—until the Reformation compounded the damage, but we will come to that.

The first consequential harm began in the decades immediately before Augustine's innovations. A brief survey of the earliest creeds may be the most economical way to pinpoint the critical digressions from one of the twin compass points with which the Original Story began: the parental nature of God. The first Christian creed, called by tradition the Apostles' Creed, presents us with few problems.

Apostles' Creed

> I believe in God the Father Almighty; Maker of heaven and earth. And in Jesus Christ His only (begotten) Son our Lord; who was conceived by the Holy Ghost, born of the Virgin Mary; suffered under Pontius Pilate, was crucified, dead, and buried; he descended into hell [Hades, spirit-world]; the third day he rose from the dead; he ascended into heaven; and sitteth at the right hand of God the Father Almighty; from thence he shall come to judge the quick and the dead. I believe in the Holy Ghost; the holy catholic Church; the communion of saints; the forgiveness of sins; the resurrection of the body [flesh]; and the life everlasting. Amen.[2]

The Apostles' Creed is the most widely accepted statement of the fundamentals of Christian belief, originating in the first

Christian centuries. It is first mentioned by name in the fourth century and was probably used as a profession of faith at baptism. Surprisingly to many Latter-day Saints, we can embrace the principles here outlined. (Our daughter, who is a member of the Church, offered to affirm this creed to qualify to enroll her daughter in a Christian primary school; her Latter-day Saint affiliation proved a barrier nonetheless.) By the standard of the Apostles' Creed, Latter-day Saints are Christian without caveats. By the fourth century, problems quickly multiply.

As we indicated in the introduction, the simplicity of a gospel message in which God's Son came to heal mankind was quickly overwhelmed by the church's arcane, philosophical disputations on the nature of the relationship between the Father and the Son. By the fourth century, the focus of theological argument was too academic for most Christians to follow. The struggle over the doctrine of the Trinity revolved around the question, Was Christ of similar, or the same, substance as the Father? The church's response was enshrined in the Nicene Creed:

Nicene Creed (excerpt)

> I believe in one God the Father Almighty; Maker of heaven and earth, and of all things visible and invisible. And in one Lord Jesus Christ, the only-begotten Son of God, begotten of the Father before all worlds [God of God], Light of Light, very God of very God, begotten, not made, being of one substance [essence] with the Father, by whom all things were made.

First formulated at the Council of Nicaea in 325, this influential creed attempted to sort out the era's controversies regarding the nature of God the Father and of Jesus Christ. A focus of debate was over the Greek term used to characterize Their relationship.

The highly arcane focus was the question, Would it be *homoiousios* (of similar substance) or *homoousios* (of the same substance)? The latter term won out, establishing a key component of Trinitarian doctrine. It is starting with the Nicene Creed that Latter-day Saints find in Christian creeds teachings that are alien to our conception of Heavenly Parents and of ourselves as children in a Divine Family. The trends first seen in the Nicene Creed became more pronounced over the next few years.

Athanasian Creed (excerpt)

> Whosoever will be saved: before all things it is necessary that he hold the Catholic [universal] Faith. . . . We worship one God in Trinity, and Trinity in Unity; neither confounding the Persons: nor dividing the Substance [essence]. For there is one Person of the Father: another of the Son: another of the Holy Ghost. But the Godhead of the father, of the Son, and of the Holy Ghost, is all one. . . . The Father incomprehensible: the Son incomprehensible: and the Holy Ghost incomprehensible. . . . And yet there are not three eternals: but one eternal. . . . So the Father is God: the Son is God: and the Holy Ghost is God. And yet there are not three Gods: but one God. . . . And in this Trinity none is afore, or after another: none is greater, or less than another. . . . But the whole three Persons are coeternal, and coequal.

Originally ascribed to Athanasius (fourth century) and now believed to have been written between the fourth and eighth centuries, this creed is a hugely influential statement of Trinitarian thought. Notice in it a further development: at this point, theology is becoming incomprehensible, reflecting belief in the incomprehensible God of Greek philosophy.

The creedal foundations of the medieval church were primarily focused on establishing the doctrine of the Trinity. That doctrine became thereafter the central defining tenet of Christianity. For example, the Act of Toleration, which the English Parliament passed in 1688, included under its umbrella of safety all dissenting Christians, as long as they did not "deny in . . . Preaching or Writing the Doctrine of the Blessed Trinity."[3] When, in the twentieth century, several mainstream churches issued statements rejecting the Latter-day Saints as a Christian faith, it was the doctrine of the Trinity they cited as explanation.[4]

To understand how the simple concept of Heavenly Parents was subjected to these convoluted and indecipherable developments, we can point to two pre-Christian sources that eventually proved decisive. Theologian Kenneth Kirk explains the first: Jewish memory, he writes, was replete with "a whole vast series of theophanies, stretching back to the dawn of [Jewish] national history. . . . Jacob had seen God face to face and lived; so too had Abraham and Moses. Isaiah had beheld the Lord high and lifted up in His temple. . . . Amos and Micah both hint at a similar vision," and so on. Under the impetus of Jewish reformers, that narrative changed dramatically, and "different expedients were adopted to secure that . . . the implication of seeing God face to face might be evaded." For example, "editors developed the habit of substituting the phrase 'appear before Jahweh' or 'be seen by Jahweh' for the phrase 'see Jahweh.'" As a consequence, when "the Old Testament canon closed[,] various influences had combined to dim the hope of the individual Jew that he should see God."[5] Drawing as the church did upon a largely Jewish convert pool, some early Christians imported these cultural predispositions.

Edwin Hatch describes a second source of similar influence. Among the original Christians, "There was no taste for metaphysical discussion: there was possibly no appreciation of metaphysical conceptions." Indeed, "the conception of the transcendence of

God is absent. God is near to men and speaks to them." Greek philosophy, however, had elevated whatever is bodiless and transcendent over whatever is physical and material. Because of the pervasive influence of Greek thought on Christianity, the Christian God became "unseen and untouched," it was believed that "he has no name," and "all anthropomorphic conceptions are explained away."[6] Typical modern-day historians continue to show greater respect for these more abstract metaphysical conceptions than for the beliefs outlined in the Apostles' Creed. For example, with remarkable condescension, Roger Olson writes that hoping to find a correct understanding of God from the earliest Christians is "expecting far too much."[7]

Augustine (354–430 AD)

The medieval creeds lay the basis for Trinitarian thought, but as Latter-day Saints we may misread that doctrine's significance. It is not the lost knowledge of God's embodiment itself that represents irreparable harm to believers. (Although as one Catholic scholar writes, "divine embodiment would have been part of the [early] theological mainstream."[8]) The real catastrophe is what is lost *when* God is disembodied. Once Christians abstract God from human form, it is natural to abstract Them from human forms of experience as well—especially of pain and suffering.[9] As one historian of religion notes matter-of-factly, "The predominant view" came to be "that God could be said to know *about* suffering, but not to *experience* this personally."[10] In the view of one theologian sympathetic to that development, "A God who suffers would be more appropriately an object of pity than of worship."[11] Augustine, the most potent, shaping voice of post-apostolic Christianity, was personally persuaded by the Greek philosophers. Speaking of God, he proclaimed, "I did not think of You under the figure of a human body. From the moment

I began to know anything of philosophy, I had rejected that idea."[12] Consequently, he also rejected as monstrous the notion that God could be personally affected by human suffering: "Who can sanely say that God is touched by any misery," he thundered.[13]

In the background of these medieval creeds, then, is the accompanying dogma that God cannot be affected by human suffering. That there is a type of love that emanates from Him might be true. But His state is not altered by, affected by, or responsive to our own condition or needs, our yearnings, our heartbreaks, or our own outpourings of love. We are convinced that any meaningful love, by contrast, implies a relationship that extends in both directions and registers a reciprocal impact: "Christ is love for this one person, this one place, this one time-bound and time-ravaged self."[14] And whatever is true of Christ, the Lord assured us, must be true of the Father (John 10:30).

Throughout the Middle Ages, however, the lamentable legacy of the creeds triumphed over a parental, feeling God. Thomas Aquinas, the second most influential voice in the shaping of Christianity affirmed, "To sorrow . . . over the misery of others belongs not to God."[15] This state of affairs, espoused by numerous theologians and prominent Christian authorities, was lamented by twentieth-century theologian Nicolas Berdyaev: "The God whom official theology tends to construct has no profound relationship with men; he is turned to stone."[16] The departure from the original Christian vision is plain: our origin as children of compassionate Heavenly Parents has been nullified.

Other fatal developments had unfolded in the late fourth century, when the focus of debate in the Christian church shifted from the Trinity to the role of human will and of God's grace in our salvation. Augustine's contemporary Pelagius, a British monk intent on reforming the moral laxity of the church in Rome, had stirred up controversy by his spirited attack on the doctrine of original sin—a doctrine championed by Augustine. An inspired Pelagius denied human depravity and argued that salvation depended in large degree on our freedom to choose between good and evil. He taught that "God, in making man in His own likeness, did not leave him 'naked and defenseless' in the face of his desires but provided him with the armaments of reason and wisdom, so that he could choose to act virtuously."[17]

In other words, "Pelagius and his followers were moral optimists. They propound that all human beings were born innocent. Infants do not enter the world with a special endowment of virtue, but neither do they carry the innate stain of vice. We possess in ourselves the possibility of choosing good over evil." But common observation shows that evil is pervasive. How to explain this? For Pelagius, evil "was essentially social: we become whoever we are largely through imitation."[18] The idea that humans have the ability to choose good over evil turns out to be precisely what King Benjamin and Paul taught, though their language has frequently confused Latter-day Saints and Christians of other denominations alike. Yes, "the natural man is an enemy to God, and will be forever and ever, unless . . . he putteth off the natural man" (Mosiah 3:19). However, moments before he spoke these words, King Benjamin had affirmed the automatic salvation of children, and in the next breath he insists it is to the state of a child (i.e., a *pre-social* being) that the natural man must return to become "a saint." Given the Augustinian view of a child as the clearest evidence of the corrupt Adamic inheritance, the difference between King Benjamin's view and Augustine's position could hardly be starker. Benjamin and Paul both teach that the state in which humans begin life is one of innocence, blamelessness. In any case, the expression *natural man* is Pauline. As Paul employs the term, it has reference to an *acquired* worldliness (one we can "put off"); it is not a statement about human ontology, inherited nature, or innate attributes. In his triple parallelism, the Apostle contrasts "the spirit of the world" with the spirit that is "of God," what "man's wisdom teacheth" with what "the Holy Ghost teacheth," and "the natural man" with "he that is spiritual" (1 Cor. 2:12–14). *Natural* is in this formulation clearly a worldly acquisition that comes from worldly wisdom and human teachings. The poet Christian Wiman put the case in words that defy the traditional Christian view but echo Restoration understanding: "Our natures—and nature itself—are not corrupt . . . but unfinished."[19] Destroying the influence of Pelagius, however, became the central preoccupation of the ultimately victorious Augustine.

At the dawn of the fifth century, Augustine unfortunately was changing his opinion about our premortal life. In his simplest early argument upholding the doctrine, he held that we look for a lost coin only if we possessed it earlier. So, too, our hunger for God must be explained as a dim recollection of what we once knew.[20] Under siege from a number of figures in the last years of the fourth century, Augustine reconsidered his support for premortality. He abandoned his defense of the doctrine, premortality began to vanish in Christian thought, and it was declared heresy soon thereafter. Forsaking premortality occurred in concert with the establishment of creation out of nothing (*creatio ex nihilo*), which took hold in this same era. In the second century, the theologian Justin Martyr had noted that the prevailing teaching was "that He in the beginning did of His goodness, for man's sake, create all things *out of unformed matter.*"[21] That doctrine of uncreated matter now fell into disfavor as well.

One modern defender of *creation ex nihilo* calls the doctrine "the lynchpin of Christianity, the truth on which theism stands or falls."[22] What difference does that make to our self-understanding as Christians? The doctrine brings in its wake several enormous consequences. For one thing, it interposes a vast distance between ourselves and God. This distance was, in fact, a deliberate intention of the idea's supporters. The influential church father Tertullian had in the second or third century expressed the fear that a soul who had an eternal past would be "on a par with God." To ensure that we remain "very far below God," Tertullian insisted that the soul is born, not eternal.[23] His emphasis reflects what has become a central tenet of Christian thought: in the words of Søren Kierkegaard, there is "an infinite, radical, qualitative difference between God and humans;"[24] according to Emil Brunner, there is "no greater sense of distance than that which lies in the words Creator-Creation. . . . Man . . . is separated by an abyss from the Divine manner of being. The greatest dissimilarity between two things which we can express at all . . . is that between the Creator and that which is created."[25]

As a result of this early-to-emerge strain of thought, the idea of what the Saints call exaltation, or *theosis*, fell into disrepute. Since antiquity, the implication had been recognized that if we had an origin among the gods, then that was our likely, even inevitable, destiny as well. Strip the human story of its origin in heaven, and the logic of the final destination is erased. To change the beginning is to change the ending. In the absence of those "heavenly courts above," where and when does the new story begin?

Once we reject a heavenly origin as exaltation-bound children of God, our beginning must lie instead in a temporal world, a purgatory into which Adam and Eve were expelled along with all their posterity. Forsaking premortality makes original sin, if not inevitable, at least more reasonable as an explanation of the human condition and human nature. And so, abandoning the understanding of life as an educative journey planned from a premortal world, Augustine refocused the story on what happened in Eden and the condition of universal sinfulness that he believed defines us: "All sin was thus Adam's first sin, and no human could escape it. How could beings so sunk in sin possibly do anything to earn themselves salvation?" So he interpreted human nature as "so trapped in sin that both body and spirit are twisted up claustrophobically without any escape."[26] And "since nothing about human beings after the Fall was worth saving, God's decision as to who should be saved was entirely arbitrary. . . . All the saved must be predestined to salvation (and . . . all the damned to damnation) before they have committed any deed of any sort."[27]

As a consequence of this new focus on universal sinfulness, Augustine diverted the entire stream of Christian thought,[28] which went from a belief in a gradual process of exaltation in which one cooperates with God, to the opposite belief in which God decrees who is saved and who is damned, independent of our choices. The claim that it was even "possible to do something about one's own salvation . . . was precisely the doctrine which Martin Luther was to make his particular target."[29] In Luther's analysis, "the only free will humankind possessed . . . was the freedom to sin."[30]

The question that should—and did—arise is this: "Why then did God create those whose fall He foreknew?" Augustine's answer: "To manifest His wrath and to demonstrate His power. Human history was the arena for this demonstration."[31] Reading such a conception of God, one can understand Thomas Jefferson's outrage at Augustine's theory: "It would be more pardonable to believe in no God at all, than to blaspheme Him by [such] atrocious attributes."[32]

Some of Augustine's contemporaries also resisted—unsuccessfully—his position: they felt these were, according to Stephen Greenblatt, "weird, uncivilized beliefs concocted by a domineering, psychologically twisted African demagogue [Augustine was from North Africa]. Should Christians, Julian of Eclanum asked, really think that a merciful, loving God would torture infants just because they were not baptized? . . . Augustine answered that yes, they are all sinners, all damned."[33] And his views, however wretched, however defamatory of both humans and God alike, carried the day. No figure in human history was more influential in the course that Christian doctrine took in the Western world. That Augustine—and the church authorities who embraced his teachings—could still profess a belief in God as the God of love, is all the proof one could need for how perversely God's "love" had come to be understood. As for Pelagius, he was accused of heresy, condemned, excommunicated, and, according to one tradition, exiled to Egypt.

One might say that at this point the rewriting of the primal story is now complete. A historian summarizes in language that Latter-day Saints can fully appreciate and applaud: the triumph of Augustine's views and the twin condemnation of Pelagius (with his defense of free will and human goodness) and of Origen (with his defense of premortal life) ensured the triumph "of a Christian theology whose central concerns were human sinfulness, not human potentiality; divine determination, not human freedom and responsibility; . . . Christianity was perhaps poorer for their suppression."[34] It was not just poorer, we would say. Christianity was now fully capable of inflicting a near universal state of "awful woundedness," creating damage from which we still suffer.

By the fourth century, God is rendered an incomprehensible entity, who created us, along with the rest of the universe, out of nothing. He is an absolute sovereign, an inaccessible father, and an enforcer of legalistic justice rather than a dispenser of bound-less compassion. His human creation sinned in the Garden, was expelled from paradise, and transmitted a guilty, sinful nature to posterity. We have no (or severely limited) free will, with a fate that was predetermined before we took our first breath. There is no question that the course of Christianity was firmly established with the triumph of Augustine over the beleaguered defenders of God's absolute love and humanity's divine potential. One historian of early Christianity summarizes the accomplishment of Augustine: the church now embraced his theology of the "eternal damnation of infants dying unbaptized, on the absolute necessity for regeneration through baptism within the Church, on the exclusive power of divine grace to save or destroy, on a form of predestination which limited the number of the saved right from the moment of creation."[35]

As a doctrine of atonement developed in the medieval period, the most sublime miracle in cosmic history was reconfigured accordingly, and so was God. Rather than Heavenly Parents who shepherd us back to Their presence in a sanctified condition, God the Father became the offended sovereign demanding recompense for His injured majesty. And so, writes Anselm, history's most influential author of Christian atonement theology (1033–1109), Christ does not come to heal but to judge. The compassion of a benevolent father "is wholly contrary to the Divine justice, which allows nothing but punishment as the recompense of sin [paid by Christ]. Therefore, as God cannot be inconsistent with Himself, His compassion cannot be of this nature."[36] In other words, "love" and "compassion" as applied to God are incomprehensible in human—or parental—terms. God's parental nature has dissolved in the face of an infinite distance. A century after Augustine, one of Christianity's most influential definitions of the Supreme Being had been reformulated by Pseudo-Dionysius from a Father to an "It": "Neither soul nor intellect; nor has it imagination, opinion, reason or understanding; nor can it be expressed or conceived, . . . ; neither is it standing, nor moving, nor at rest; neither has it power nor is power, nor is light; neither does it live nor is it life; . . . nor is it subject to intelligible contact; nor is it spirit according to our understanding, nor filiation, nor paternity."[37]

The historian Brinley Rees assesses Augustine's far-reaching impact: Though he was surely "one of the most loving of men and well-loved by others, [he became] so obsessed with the idea of God's power that he left little room for His love."[38]

Reformation (sixteenth century)

In the common Latter-day Saint retelling, a little more than a thousand years after the triumph of Augustine's views, the Reformation shines as a great light in the darkness, paving the way for the Restoration. The facts are rather otherwise. Gutenberg begins commercial printing with moveable type in 1440, and within decades, in countries across Europe that are outside of Catholic control, Bibles are appearing in vernacular languages. That positive development is an essential chapter in the emerging story of religious freedom and pluralism. However, the actual doctrinal changes ushered in by the Reformation almost without exception further compound the darkness of the long night. The reason is simple, and the evidence extensive.

In 1506, for the first time, Augustine's body of work is published in a complete, scholarly edition.[39] When it is studied by Luther and his contemporaries, it creates a theological shock-wave. Augustine's focus on original sin, depravity, and a severely constrained human will is given renewed emphasis to the further diminishment of confidence in innate goodness, human potential, and the exercise of moral freedom. One historian says that Luther's project—which spread to the other Reformers—was nothing other than reviving in a more concentrated form Augustine's "radical pessimism about humanity's capacity for salvation."[40] This revolution has been more narrowly summarized by the historian B. B. Warfield: "The Reformation, inwardly considered, was just the ultimate triumph of Augustine's doctrine of grace."[41] That doctrine represents a complete rewriting of the Original Story, and it is based on Augustine's misreading of what it means to be saved, or in his term, "justified." This is how it happens: "The word 'justification' . . . in Latin literally means *the making of* someone *to be* righteous. In Luther's understanding it meant the *declaring* of someone to be righteous: God 'imputes' the merits of the crucified and risen Christ through grace to a fallen human being, who remains without inherent merit and who, without this 'imputation,' would remain unrighteous."[42] Christ does not transform us, in other words. He simply *declares* us righteous, and therefore "saved."

In his translation of the book of Romans, Luther inserts a word that renders Augustine's position on grace to be incompatible with personal effort. Romans 3:28 holds that "man is justified . . . by faith." In Luther's Bible, we read that "man is justified by faith *only*." The "only" was Luther's addition—it is not in the Greek text.[43] When challenged on his addition, Luther responded, "I know very well that the word *solum* is not in the Greek or Latin texts. . . . If your papist wants to make so much fuss about the word *sola* (alone) tell him this, 'Dr. Martin Luther will have it so.'"

Christ's role, to recall Schleiermacher's words with which we began this book, has been reduced to incoherence. No longer are we divine souls engaged on a journey planned from before creation, being schooled through the educative experiences of mortality, gradually growing into beings like our Divine Parents. Instead, we are merely human detritus of an Adamic catastrophe, saved or damned as God wills through an "imputed" righteousness.

Along with a newly defined "grace," Augustine's many other positions now receive renewed emphasis and reinforcement as dogmas in the Protestant Reformation. Though few of us may be aware of his enduring influence, it is the case that "Luther's ideas . . . have found their most fertile ground in America."[44] American religious culture is almost entirely Lutheran and Calvinist in its roots. "One of the most important consequences of the European Reformation," writes Massey, was "the export of a militant form of English Protestantism to north America."[45] Was this a prelude to the Restoration?

When Joseph heard God level His assessment of the state of nineteenth-century Christianity, it was "their creeds" God singled out for particular condemnation. Contrary to Latter-day Saint mythology, it was not the Catholic creeds of the medieval church that drew forth God's ire. It is unlikely that Joseph would have even been familiar with words or names like Nicaea or Chalcedon or Athanasius or Arias. What Joseph did have to say about

Catholicism was largely positive: "The old Catholic church is worth more than all" the other sects, he said in his last recorded sermon.[46] No wonder: Joseph saw manifold parallels between Restoration teachings and Catholic belief. One of the most stubborn myths in the Restoration Church is the notion that the Protestant Reformation was a kind of preparatory step toward the Restoration, when in fact the opposite is true.[47]

There is no indication that Joseph heard *Catholic* when the Lord warned of the lasting damage of the creeds, nor are those Catholic teachings suggested when almost twenty years later, Joseph was still telling the Saints of the "confusion" sown by those same "creeds" that were "riveted . . . upon the hearts of the children" (D&C 123:7). By contrast, how did the creeds and revised prayer books of Joseph's *Protestant* world sow confusion that still afflicts so many Latter-day Saints?

The Augsburg Confession–1530 (excerpts)

Produced in 1530, the Augsburg Confession was the definitive creed of the Lutheran Church. As explicitly alluded to previously, the Reformation under Luther was to a large degree the positioning at the center of theology Augustine's writings on grace, especially his emphasis on original sin, depravity, and the absence of . . . free will, as most people would understand that term:

> All men . . . are conceived and born in sin. That is, all men are full of evil lust and inclinations from their mother's wombs and are unable by nature to have true fear of God and true faith in God. Moreover, this inborn sickness and hereditary sin is truly sin.

> . . . We concede that all men have free will. . . . [If by that term we mean the freedom "to eat or dress" as we please.

But such freedom does not extend to the choice to serve God or oppose Him].

The Book of Common Prayer–1549/1552

The Book of Common Prayer is the manual used in all Anglican church services. The 1549 Catholic version included such prayers as "Grant . . . that at the day of judgment his soul and all the souls of thy elect, departed out of this life, may with us and we with them, fully receive thy promises."[48] The Protestant revision of 1552 removed all prayers offered on behalf of the dead because they "smacked of the old religion in which the living could perform religious acts on behalf of the dead."[49]

Latter-day Saints may not see an immediate connection between prayers for the dead and our own temple work. But notice what underlying paradigm they share, one that is abandoned by the Protestant creeds: Saints believe in a porous membrane joining heaven and earth, which allows us to affect the welfare of the dead, and they ours. And we believe that from the beginnings of the everlasting covenant, we are all in a shared endeavor, working for each other's progress now and forever. Death does not impose impermeable walls that separate us, nor is it the end of our striving.

The Westminster Confession–1648 (excerpts)

Approved by the English Parliament in 1648, the Westminster Confession establishes the basis of Reformed theology, which was embraced by the Anglicans, by the Puritans in England and the American colonies, and by the Presbyterians. It also served as basis for the Baptist creeds and, with minor modifications, was adopted by the Congregationalists and later the Methodists. The Westminster Confession was the creed with which Joseph Smith and his contemporaries would have been most familiar:

The Holy Scriptures [are] most necessary; those former ways
of God's revealing His will unto His people being now ceased
. . . , unto which nothing at any time is to be added . . . by
new revelations. . . .

There is but one only living and true God, who is infinite in
being and perfection, a most pure spirit, invisible, without
body, parts, or passions; . . .

He is the alone foundation of all being. . . .

God from all eternity did, by the most wise and holy counsel
of His own will, freely and unchangeably ordain whatsoever
comes to pass. . . .

By the decree of God, for the manifestation of His glory,
some men and angels are predestinated unto everlasting life,
and others foreordained to everlasting death. . . .

By this sin [our first parents] fell from their original righteousness and communion with God, and so became dead
in sin, and wholly defiled in all the parts and faculties of
soul and body. They being the root of all mankind, the
guilt of this sin was imputed; and the same death in sin,
and corrupted nature, conveyed to all their posterity de-
scending from them.

With this creedal development, the future gulf between
the Latter-day Saints and other Protestant branches is magnified
enormously. In some cases, this Confession brought new emphases
in creedal Christianity to the fore; in other cases, new doctrinal
developments are even further removed from the original gospel.
Crucial ways in which Latter-day Saint doctrine differs from the
doctrine declared in the Westminster Confession include the
following:

- Latter-day Saints espouse an open, rather than a closed, canon, along with the principle of continuing revelation.

- Latter-day Saints embrace a God who has a physical body and—most emphatically—passions, that is, the capacity to be moved to grief by the pain of another. The dominant trend through most of the Christian centuries had been to see God as having no anthropomorphic form and as incapable of suffering in sympathy with humankind (despite occasional voices that had emerged to challenge both tenets). With the Westminster Confession, however, a bodiless and passionless God became explicit dogma for Protestants.

- Latter-day Saints reject *creation ex nihilo*, believing that God organized the universe out of eternally existing matter. While *creation ex nihilo* had long been dominant in Christian thought, Calvin pushed this belief to appalling lengths. In claiming that God is the "source of all that is," Calvin stipulates that God ordains all events, historical and personal, tragic and horrific, that unfold in human history. Calvin's God does not merely foresee and permit all that transpires; as Sovereign, He personally planned and orchestrated the entirety of history. In Calvin's view, all events are in God's blueprint, including "the fall of the first man and in him the ruin of his posterity," which God "at His own pleasure arranged." In Luther's language, "nothing takes place but as [God] wills it."[50] God "foresees, purposes, and does all things according to His immutable, eternal, and infallible will. By this thunderbolt, 'Free-will' is thrown prostrate and utterly dashed to pieces."[51]

- Latter-day Saints emphatically reject the doctrines of predestination as they pertain to human destinies. Human beings are "free forever, . . . free to choose liberty and eternal life . . . or to choose captivity and death" (2 Ne. 2:26–27).

- Finally, we believe humankind does not inherit the sin or guilt of Adam and is not inherently good or evil but, rather, innocent (D&C 93:38). Though we all inhabit a mortal condition with its earthly desires and propensities, total depravity and deadness to all good are not accurate characterizations of human nature.

- The sum total of the Reformation's creedal developments were criticized by the Catholic humanist Erasmus (1466–1536) and affirmed by Luther. Erasmus protested this new version of God, who seemed "to delight in the torments of the miserable, and to be an object of hatred rather than of love." In response to Erasmus's complaint, Luther wrote, "This is the highest degree of faith—to believe he is merciful, who saves so few and damns so many; to believe him just, who according to His own will, makes us necessarily damnable."[52]

In our own era, the leading physicist Steven Weinberg noted the logical implications of such belief: "With or without religion, good people can behave well and bad people can do evil. But for good people to do evil—that takes religion."[53]

Aftermath

Our intention in reviewing this history is not to cast aspersions on men or movements of the past that shaped the Christian past; in most cases, the Reformers were motivated by legitimate concerns about abuses and doubtful doctrines of the institutional church of their day. However, as we have tried to indicate, in this process of Reform they often compounded the slanders against our Heavenly Parents and Their designs, in spite of a number of salutary developments across Christian thought in more recent times. And it may well be, as a modern theologian states, that "most of us today have traveled far enough from Augustine and

Calvin to believe that the heavenly Father of Jesus's teaching *wants* to save all men."[54] Our point is that those formative ideas of the Reformation are so deeply embedded in our Christian past and consciousness that there is likely a connection between this history and the roots of much of our "awful woundedness" that runs so deep today. For example, one historian emphasizes that "the concept of hell did not just survive in antebellum America: it thrived. It saturated private and public discourse. . . . Why,"she goes on to ask, "did so many Americans frame their concerns about themselves and their friends, families, nation and world in terms of divine punishment and everlasting torment?"[55] As examples of this legacy that stretches back centuries, we could note the following:

- In the eighteenth century, Jonathan Edwards gave his famous "Sinners in the Hands of an Angry God" sermon. "The God that holds you over the pit of hell, much as one holds a spider, or some loathsome insect over the fire, abhors you, and is dreadfully provoked: His wrath towards you burns like fire; he looks upon you as worthy of nothing else, but to be cast into the fire." Modern apologists often deny that that sermon was typical of Edwards or of the harsh Calvinism he preached. However, Edwards gave the sermon repeatedly, generally achieving the same effect: "They [his audience] suddenly realized they are horribly doomed. 'Before the sermon was done . . . there was a great moaning and crying throughout the whole house. What shall I do to be saved. Oh I am going to Hell. . . . Shrieks and cries were piercing and amazing.'"[56]

- An eighteenth-century anthology used by thousands of Americans depicted a Christian who agonized over "the vast uncertainty I am struggling with . . . the force and vivacity of my apprehensions; every doubt wears the face of horror, and would perfectly overwhelm me, but for some faint gleams of hope, which dart across the tremendous gloom. What tongue can utter the anguish of a soul suspended between the extremes of infinite joy or eternal misery. . . . I tremble and shudder."[57]

- By the nineteenth century, the link between religious trauma and clinical mental illness was becoming well established. Researchers "found religious anxiety to be a leading cause of insanity." One study determined that out of the various causes, "religious anxiety was number one by a three-fold factor." Another physician wrote about suicide due to religious "melancholy," noting that the traumatic fear of imminent damnation "is not infrequent in this country."[58]

- One of the nineteenth century's most popular preachers relied on "terror, guilt and shame." He threatened that at the Judgment, "husbands and wives will have to testify against their spouses. Parents will see their unsaved children swept to hell for reasons directly attributable to themselves."[59]

- Summarizing the impact of what one scholar calls the founding of "militant Protestantism" of this country,[60] another historian notes that "the marriage of religion and fear in the United States" is a prevalent one. In this "religion of fear," "tales of terror have long served civic purposes in this haunted nation."[61]

These trends were not universal, but they were pervasive and continue to manifest themselves, even in our own religious tradition. One could read Elder Dieter Uchtdorf's words as a commentary on this long and tragic history of discourse: "It is true that fear can have a powerful influence over our actions and behavior. But that influence tends to be temporary and shallow. Fear rarely has the power to change our hearts. . . . People who are fearful may say and do the right things, but they do not feel the right things."[62]

The Contemporary Scene

And in the present moment? We may not be taking our own lives out of fear of damnation, or shrieking in the church aisles (from boredom, maybe, but not terror), but various forms of damage across the spiritual and emotional spectrum raise the question of what role, for good and for ill, religious language and paradigms exert. Trauma and woundedness take many forms. But much healing takes one. Huston Smith writes in reference to the early Christians, "The only power that can effect transformations of the order we have described is love. . . . Imagination may fail us here, but logic need not. If we felt loved, not abstractly or in principle but vividly and personally, by one who unites all power and perfection, the experience could melt our fear, guilt, and self- concern permanently." As Kierkegaard said, "If at every moment both present and future I were certain that nothing has happened or can ever happen that would separate us from the infinite love of [God], that would be the reason for joy."[63] And we can know, as Paul did, that nothing, "neither death, nor life, nor angels, nor principalities, nor powers, nor things present, nor things to come, nor height, nor depth, nor any other creature, shall be able to separate us from the love of God" (Rom. 8:38–39).

Might reordering our religious language to be more consistent with this love known to the first Christians at least help to address our unprecedented rates of depression, anxiety, divorce, suicide, alcoholism, addiction, and other mental health issues? Recent data reveals how much we are struggling in our modern world:

- Between 2005 and 2017, the proportion of teens ages twelve to seventeen who reported the symptoms of a major depressive episode within the last year rose from 8.7 percent to 13.2 percent, data showed. Adults ages eighteen to twenty-five showed similar trends.[64]

- In a 2017 survey of nearly forty-eight thousand college students, 64 percent said they had felt "very lonely" in the previous twelve months, while only 19 percent reported that they never felt lonely, according to the American College Health Association. Students also reported feeling "overwhelming anxiety" (62 percent) or feeling "very sad" (69 percent), and that "things were hopeless" (53 percent). Nearly 12 percent of these students had seriously considered suicide.[65]

- "Some scientists now believe that extreme feelings of guilt in children . . . can be a strong warning sign for mental disorders such as depression, anxiety, obsessive-compulsive disorder (OCD), and bipolar disorder later on in life. Research has long linked excessive feelings of guilt to mental disorders in adults—the DSM-V (*Manual of Mental Disorders*) lists feelings of excessive guilt as a symptom for depression."[66]

In the twenty-first century, something novel has crept over the horizon of contemporary maladies, creating a new landscape. Ross Douthat notes that the statistics alone don't tell the whole story. While it is true that "teenagers in the Internet age are more stressed out, more anxiety ridden, more prone to depression than teenagers in the more dangerous past," the larger picture our world presents is one in which there is a general, almost universal "tranquilization" of life. Youth today are "the most medicated generation in history" (which is not to say that much of it is not medically warranted). Tellingly, the most popular drugs, whether prescribed or illicit, "are designed to be calming, relaxing, offering a smoothed-out experience rather than a spiky high." Even the opioid epidemic is a new kind of drug pandemic, one that "quiets rather than inflames."[67] Andrew Sullivan summarizes the common feature in all of the above: "The drugs now conquering America are downers: they are not the means to engage in life more vividly but to seek a respite from its ordeals."[68]

Another symptom reveals the same underlying crisis: the higher education push for "safe zones," trigger warnings, and a generally flattened and inoffensive marketplace of ideas. Greater empathy and sensitivity are wonderful developments, as long as they do not encourage a desperate escapism masquerading as a freedom without historical precedent: "the freedom to be 'safe'—broadly defined."[69] ("We were willing to *know* hurt," Francine Bennion reminds us.[70]) It seems reasonable to suspect that the craving for safety in all its forms is a factor in that ideological insularity, retreat into microcommunities, and unprecedented social and political polarization that are so incompatible with the open-hearted Zion communities we are called to construct.

History and social science alike conclude that, in the words of the angel, our modern society is in a state of "awful woundedness." And the angel addressing Nephi tied at least some of that woundedness afflicting our world to our religious inheritance. Presumably, as beneficiaries of the restored "plain and precious things," we as members of the Church of Jesus Christ of Latter-day Saints have the antidote, the healing balm for some of the general condition of spiritual and emotional impairment. And often, that proves to be the case. Yet many Saints, a few of whom shared their thoughts in our opening pages, are wondering how it is possible for the restored Church to inflict or add injury rather than proffer the balm of Gilead. Why can Church attendance create as much unease as it can solace? Why do we not, as Brigham Young recognized, more often "enjoy the spirit" of the gospel we profess? In what follows, we want to suggest very specific ways in which our language continues to bear the traces of the injurious legacy we tracked previously. As Saints we rely upon scripture and revelation as our spiritual guides—and much of our hurt is related to both. As one member wrote us, "My own mental well-being required a path of gentleness, love, and understanding. The scriptures weren't always helpful in this process." So let us first consider the place of those resources in our spiritual journey.

NOTES

1   Diana Butler Bass, *A People's History of Christianity: The Other Side of the Story* (New York: HarperCollins, 1989; HarperOne, 2010), 17.

2   All versions of the creeds and confessions in this section are from Philip Schaff, ed., *The Creeds of Christendom with a History and Critical Notes*, 6th edition (Grand Rapids: Baker Book House, 1990).

3   An Act for Exempting their Majestyes Protestant Subjects dissenting from the Church of England from the Penalties of certaine Lawes, 1688. Cited in Terryl Givens, *Wrestling the Angel: The Foundations of Mormon Thought* (New York: Oxford University Press, 2015), 69.

4   In May of 2000 the United Methodist Church passed a resolution asserting that the Church of Jesus Christ of Latter-day Saints "does not fit within the bounds of the historic, apostolic tradition of Christian faith." First cited by way of explanation was the Church's "radically differing doctrine on . . . the nature and being of God." The Presbyterian Church (USA) and the Southern Baptist Convention passed similar resolutions, followed by the Vatican, which in 2001 declared Latter-day Saint baptisms invalid. See Terryl Givens, *Wrestling the Angel*, 69.

5   Kenneth Kirk, *The Vision of God: The Christian Doctrine of the Summum Bonum* (New York: Harper, 1932), 11–14.

6   Edwin Hatch, *The Influence of Greek Ideas on Christianity* (New York: Harper & Row, 1957; repr., Gloucester, MA: Peter Smith, 1970), 251–52.

7   Roger E. Olson, *The Story of Christian Theology* (Downers Grove, IL: InterVarsity Press, 1999), 52.

8   Stephen Webb, *Jesus Christ, Eternal God: Heavenly Flesh and the Metaphysics of Matter* (New York: Oxford University Press, 2012), 249.

9   This point has been made by theologian Marcel Sarot. To believe that God *can* suffer, he argues, is to "accept that God is, in a sense embodied." He has written an entire book on that linkage. *God, Passibility, and Corporeality* (Kampen, Netherlands: Kok Pharos, 1992), 9.

10   Alister McGrath, *Heresy: A History of Defending the Truth* (New York: HarperOne, 2010), 25.

11   Richard Creel in Internet Encyclopedia of Philosophy, s.v. "Western Concepts of God," by Brian Morley, accessed, August 12, 2020, https://www .iep.utm.edu/god-west/#SH3h. See also Creel's Divine Impassibility: An Essay in Philosophical Theology (Eugene, OR: Wipf and Stock, 1985).

12   Augustine, *Confessions* 7.1, trans. F. J. Sheed (Indianapolis: Hackett, 2006), 117.

13   Augustine, *De Diversis Quaestionibus ad Simplicianum* 2, in Nicolas Wolterstorff, "Suffering Love," in *Augustine's Confessions: Critical Essays*, ed. William E. Mann (Lanham, MD: Rowan and Littlefield, 2006), 122.

14   Christian Wiman, *My Bright Abyss* (New York: Farrar, Straus and Giroux, 2014), 121.

15   Thomas Aquinas, *Summa Theologica*, question 21, article 3 (Chicago: Encyclopedia Britannica, 1980), 1:126.

16   Marie-Madaleine Davy, *Nicolas Berdyaev: Man of the Eighth Day* (London: Geoffrey Bles, 1967), 62–63.

17   Michael Massing, *Fatal Discord: Erasmus, Luther, and the Fight for the Western Mind* (New York: HarperCollins, 2018), 134.

18   Stephen Greenblatt, *The Rise and Fall of Adam and Eve* (New York: Norton, 2017), 105.

19   Wiman, *My Bright Abyss*, 103.

20   See Terryl Givens, *When Souls Had Wings: Pre-Mortal Existence in Western Thought* (New York: Oxford University Press, 2010), 99–128.

21   Justin Martyr, *The First Apology* 10, in *The Ante-Nicene Fathers* [hereafter *ANF*], ed. Alexander Roberts and James Donaldson (Grand Rapids: Eerdmans, 1977*)*, 1:165.

22   Givens, *Wrestling*, 53

23   Tertullian, *Treatise on the Soul* 24, in *ANF* 3:203.

24   Søren Kierkegaard, *Journals and Papers* (Bloomington: Indiana University Press, 1967), 2:113, quoted in Merold Westphal, *Kierkegaard's Concept of Faith* (Grand Rapids, MI: Eerdmans, 2014), 136.

25 Emil Brunner, *Man in Revolt*, trans. Olive Wyon (London: Lutter-worth Press, 1953), 90.

26 Diarmaid MacCulloch, *The Reformation: A History* (New York: Viking, 2004), 118.

27 MacCulloch, *Reformation* 106.

28 A growing chorus of scholars now acknowledges that Augustine was more the innovator than defender of Christian orthodoxy. His still-maligned opponent, Pelagius, had good reason to consider himself "a traditionalist, defending the true faith against the innovations of Augustine." Henry Chadwick, *Early Christian Thought and the Classical Tradition* (Oxford Clarendon Press, 1966), 907, quoted in B. R. Rees, *Pelagius: Life and Letters* (Woodbridge, UK: Boydell, 1991), 132.

29 MacCulloch, *Reformation*, 14.

30 Richard Marius, *Martin Luther: The Christian Between God and Death* (Cambridge, MA: Harvard University Press, 2009), 197.

31 Augustine's reply is from his *Literal Commentary on Genesis*, cited in Jaroslav Pelikan, *The Emergence of the Catholic Tradition* (Chicago: University of Chicago Press, 1971), 297.

32 Kathryn Gin Lum, *Damned Nation: Hell in America from the Revolution to Reconstruction* (New York: Oxford University Press, 2014), 18.

33 Greenblatt, *Rise and Fall*, 107.

34 Elizabeth A. Clark, *The Origenist Controversy: The Cultural Construction of an Early Christian Debate* (Princeton: Princeton University Press, 1992), 250.

35 B. R. Rees, *Pelagius: Life and Letters* (Woodbridge, UK: Boydell, 1991), 17.

36 Anselm, *Cur Deus Homo* (Fort Worth: RDMc Publishing, 1903), 77.

37 Arthur Versluis, *Magic and Mysticism: An Introduction to Western Esoteric Traditions* (London: Rowman and Littlefield, 2007), 42.

38 Rees, *Pelagius*, 47.

39 The work was by the Basel printer Johnannes Amerbach. See Massing, *Fatal Discord*, 128.

40 MacCulloch, *Reformation*, 134.

41 B. B. Warfield, *Calvin and Augustine* (Philadelphia, 1956), 332. Cited in MacCulloch, *Reformation*, 108.

42 MacCulloch, *Reformation*, 115.

43 Martin Luther, "On Translating: An Open Letter," in *Selected Writ-*

ings of Martin Luther, ed. Theodore G. Tappert (Minneapolis: Fortress Press, 2007): 4:180, 177. Some previous Catholic translations had also added the word, it should be pointed out, but without erecting an entire new theology on that basis.

44 Massing, *Fatal Discord*, xxii.

45 MacCulloch, *Reformation*, xxiv.

46 Andrew F. Ehat and Lyndon W. Cook, *The Words of Joseph Smith* (Orem, UT: Grandin Book Company, 1991), 381–82.

47 Following are the three most conspicuous parallels between Restoration teachings and Catholic belief, which are also out of harmony with Protestant developments:

(1) Contrary to the idea of salvation as the "imputation" of righteousness, Catholics saw salvation as a process in which the will must be fully engaged. Cardinal John Henry Newman said, "Good works . . . are required, not as if they had any merit of their own, nor as if they could . . . purchase heaven for us." But through "our acts of charity, self-denial, and forbearance" we will become "charitable, self-denying, and forbearing. . . . These holy works will be the means of making our hearts holy, and of preparing us for the future presence of God." John Henry Newman, *Selection, Adapted to the Seasons of the Ecclesiastical Year* (London: Longmans, Green, 1895), 282.

(2) Joseph believed the greatest deficits in Christianity, and a culminating aim of the Restoration, were the sacraments, ordinances, and covenants of the gospel, administered by divine authority. Catholics, of course, have always believed in a priesthood authority that descends from the apostles, and that adds efficacy to sacramental acts. A first principle of Luther was that "whatever comes out of the water of baptism is already a consecrated priest." Ordination to a priesthood was "the first wall of Jericho" in need of overthrow. And virtually all Protestants denied that sacraments are essential to salvation, believing instead that the sacraments serve as signs and symbols only. Martin Luther, "To the Christian Nobility," in *Selected Writings of Martin Luther*, ed. Theodore G. Tappert (Minneapolis: Fortress Press, 2007), 1:263, 265.

(3) Joseph's dominant preoccupation throughout his life and ministry was to connect the disparate realms of the living and the dead, uniting both in eternal bonds of love. The Catholics had an extensive theological tradition that linked the actions of the living to the condition of the deceased, including prayers and masses offered on their behalf. Protestants were determined to eradicate any connection or concern that moved beyond the grave. Calvin taught that even "commending [the dead] to [God's] grace" was unscriptural

and inappropriate. Bruce Gordon, *Calvin* (New Haven: Yale University Press, 2009), 255. Protestants entirely dismissed "the fatal idea that in some way the living could influence the fate of the departed, [as it] flew in the face of the evangelical insistence on God's grace as the sole determinant of human salvation." Diarmaid MacCulloch, *Thomas Cranmer: A Life* (New Haven: Yale University Press, 1996), 509. When Joseph restored vicarious baptism for the dead, effecting a chain of influence between the two realms, critics were quick to see the parallels with Catholic beliefs. "You are as bad as the papists," they said. Rather than deny the similarity, the Latter-day Saint editor Thomas Ward responded: "We believe, that fallen as the Roman church may be, she has traces of many glorious principles that were once in the church of Christ, of which . . . the protestant world knows nothing." Truly, as an admiring Catholic scholar noted, Joseph Smith "was, in a way, reinventing Catholicism for a time and a place that did not have access to a truly Catholic presence." Sean Salai, S. J., "Catholic and Mormon: Author Q&A with Professor Stephen H. Webb," *America: The National Catholic Review*, http://americamagazine.org/content /all-things/catholic-and-mormon-author-qa-professor-stephenh-webb.

48 *The Book of Common Prayer*, 1549 edition, http://justus.anglican .org/resources/BCp/1549/Burial_1549.htm.

49 Mark Chapman, *Anglicanism: A Very Short Introduction* (New York: Oxford, 2006), 26.

50 Massing, *Fatal Discord*, 674.

51 Martin Luther, *The Bondage of the Will* (Peabody, MA: Hendrickson, 2008), 33.

52 Martin Luther (quoting Erasmus) in *Bondage of the Will*, 55.

53 Steven Weinberg, "A Designer Universe?" Physics and Astronomy Online, accessed August 12, 2020, https://www.physlink.com/Education /essay_weinberg.cfm.

54 J. Hick, *Death and Eternal Life* (London: Collins, 1976), 450, cited in Rees, *Pelagius, Life*, 47.

55 Lum, *Damned Nation*, 3

56 George Marsden, *Jonathan Edwards: A Life* (New Haven: Yale University Press, 2004), 220.

57 Arthur Masson, ed., *A Collection of English Prose and Verse for the Use of Schools*, 7th ed. (Edinburgh: 1773), 196.

58 Lum, *Damned Nation*, 119–20, 270.

59 Lum, *Damned Nation*, 43.

60 MacCulloch, *Reformation*, xxii.

61 Jason G. Bivins, *Religion of Fear: The Politics of Horror in Conservative Evangelicalism* (Oxford: Oxford University Press, 2008), 16.

62 Dieter F. Uchtdorf, "Perfect Love Casteth Out Fear," *Ensign* 47, no. 5 (May 2017): 105.

63 Huston Smith, *The World's Religions* (New York: HarperCollins, 1991), 334–35.

64 Evie Blad, "Schools Grapple with Student Depression as Data Show Problem Worsening," Education Week, March 14, 2019, https://www.edweek .org/ew/articles/2019/03/14/schools-grapple-with-student-depression-as-data .html.

65 "Fact Sheet: Loneliness on Campus," The UnLonely Project, The Foundation for Art & Healing, accessed August 12, 2020, https://artandhealing .org/campus-loneliness-fact-sheet/.

66 Jenny Chen, "Childhood Guilt, Adult Depression?" *The Atlantic*, January 5, 2015, https://www.theatlantic.com/health/archive/2015/01/childhood -guilt-adult-depression/384176/.

67 Ross Douthat, *The Decadent Society: How We Became the Victims of Our Own Success* (New York: Avid Reader, 2020), 126.

68 Andrew Sullivan, "The Poison We Pick," *New York Magazine*, quoted in Douthat, *Decadent Society*, 127.

69 Douthat *Decadent Society*, 141.

70 Francine R. Bennion, "A Latter-day Saint Theology of Suffering," in *At the Pulpit*, ed. Jennifer Reeder and Kate Holbrook (Salt Lake City: Church Historian's Press, 2017), 224.

CHAPTER THREE

Modern Liahonas

Scripture, Revelation, and Disciples of the Second Sort

Two sources of truth that are available to us are revelation (prophetic and personal) and scripture (traditional Christian and Restoration). In the latter source in particular, we find an immediate complication—the same complication Joseph Smith discovered in his original quest for enlightenment. Protestants based their claim to truth and authority on one source, the Bible alone (*sola scriptura*). The Church of Jesus Christ of Latter-day Saints, by contrast, could be said to have begun with a pointed and emphatic rejection of *sola scriptura*. The entire possibility of a biblically based Christianity is rendered incoherent in Joseph Smith's personal experience, which was his—and his movement's—entire rationale for a newly revealed religion. As Joseph said of his personal quest, "Teachers of religion of the different sects understood the same passage of Scripture so differently as to *destroy all confidence in settling the question [of religious truth] by an appeal to the Bible*" (our emphasis).[1] A historian of the Reformation found himself in agreement: "Ideas mattered profoundly; they had an independent power of their own, and they could be corrosive and destructive. The most corrosive ideas of all were to be found in the Bible, an explosive, unpredictable force in every age."[2]

How then do we find our way to clarity when Latter-day Saint canonical works can provide similar bases for disputation and disagreement? We can begin by recognizing that the tender in heart have long had difficulty in parsing the scriptures to find a true portrait of God. One early Christian so despaired of reconciling the gentle Christ of the New Testament with the vengeful figure of the Old Testament that he advocated abandoning the Jewish scriptures altogether. Marcion (85–160 AD) and many other Christians found it impossible to reconcile what they saw as two versions of God and proposed eliminating the Old Testament from the Christian canon. The great twentieth-century scholar and theologian Adolf von Harnack actually suggested that we might follow Marcion's proposal to make Christianity more self-consistent.[3]

A few centuries after Marcion, the inspired Christian ascetic Isaac the Syrian was wrestling with the same problem. He did not reject the Old Testament but questioned its inerrancy: "To suppose that retribution for evil acts is to be found in [God] is abominable."[4] Readers who aspire to find perfect consistency across the standard works will find that they are on a fool's errand. For example, Francine Bennion has pointed out that one can read in the story of Jephthah sacrificing his daughter for victory in war (Judges 11) a "version of God . . . who can and must be bargained with; a God who considers unquestioned obedience to be the highest good—not just the *means* to goodness but goodness itself; a God who causes suffering in the innocent and also authorizes theology that fosters it." However, she notes, such a reading is in direct tension with "other scriptures that seem to speak of God's valuing agency above obedience, love above tradition, and the human heart above ritual sacrifice."[5]

One cannot even read the opening passages of Matthew 1 and Luke 3 without encountering contradictory genealogies for Jesus. In Matthew and Luke, Jesus proclaims that neutrality to Him is opposition: "He who is not with me is *against* me" (Matt. 12:30; Luke 11:23; our emphasis). In Mark and elsewhere in Luke, He teaches the reverse, that neutrality is tacit support: "Whoever is not against me is *for* me" (Mark 9:40; Luke 9:50; our emphasis). In the book of Joshua we read that in his conquest Joshua "left no survivor, but he utterly destroyed all who breathed" (Josh. 11:15). In Judges, we read of the Israelites asking the Lord who should lead the attack against the very Canaanites Joshua had presumably entirely eradicated (Judg. 1:1). All these and myriad other contradictions have their fierce apologists finding creative ways of reconciling apparent disharmonies, even though some difficulties are frankly insurmountable. (The author of the Gospel of John tells us quite clearly that the Last Supper occurs the day *before* Passover; the three other writers all state that it occurs *on* Passover).

Nevertheless, the drive to find scriptural consistency is fiercely embedded in much of the Protestant tradition: Evangelicals who subscribe to the Chicago Statement on Biblical Inerrancy believe that "being wholly and verbally God-given, Scripture is without error or fault in all its teaching . . . in what it states about God's acts in creation, about the events of world history, and about its own literary origins under God." Furthermore, "the whole of Scripture and all its parts, down to the very words of the original, were given by divine inspiration. We deny that the inspiration of Scripture can rightly be affirmed of the whole without the parts, or of some parts but not the whole." As for human and cultural influence on the way such revelation is received, the statement rejects those factors: "We further deny that the corruption of human culture and language through sin has thwarted God's work of inspiration."[6]

If friends of other faiths were to attend a typical Latter-day Saint Sunday School class, they would be excused for thinking that the Saints also subscribe to the claims made in the Chicago Statement. The prevailing assumption within Latter-day Saint culture, apparent in virtually all scriptural exegesis, is that we can make all the scriptures harmonize; everything therein is a true and accurate account of God's nature and dealings, including God's murder of the "lads" who mocked Elisha (2 Kgs. 2:23–24), God's massacre of Egyptian children (Ex. 11–12), and His explicit directive to stone to death the Sabbath stick-gatherer (Num. 15:35). Can we actually reconcile Jehovah's genocide of the Canaanites—and His smiting of thousands because David took a census—with that same Jehovah's compassion for the sparrow? Are we also content to accept God's killing of Uzza, who tried to protect the sacred ark from tumbling and was killed for his efforts (2 Sam. 6:7)?

It is an observable fact that we are not, in general, approaching scriptural reading in the light of core Restoration teachings that advise us to be cautious in our assumptions about scriptural inerrancy. The entire Restoration was a project intended to redress the state of "awful woundedness" that was explicitly attributed to scriptural corruption and the loss of the Bible's "plain and precious things" (1 Ne. 13:32). No wonder, then, that the first prophet of the Restoration reported that there were "*many* things in the Bible which do not . . . accord with the revelation of the holy Ghost to me."[7]

As for the role of our simple humanity and cultural conditioning in scriptural fallibility, George Q. Cannon took a position on divine revelation that is precisely opposite to the Chicago Statement: "The revelation we may get, imperfect at times because of our fallen condition and because of our failure to comprehend the nature of it, comes from God. . . . Man is but the medium, but the instrument, is the conduit through which it flows. . . . This is the position occupied by the Latter-day Saints. We believe in revelation. It may come dim; it may come indistinct; it may come sometimes with a degree of vagueness which we do not like. Why? Because of our imperfection; because we are not prepared to receive it as it comes in its purity; in its fulness from God. He is not to blame for this."[8] What is true of revelation in general must be true of scripture in particular, as scripture is one form that revelation takes.

Brigham Young's concerns mirrored those of Joseph Smith and George Cannon, except that Young went much further than most all of his peers and fellow Christians:

> I have heard some make the broad assertion that every word within the lids of the Bible was the word of God. I have said to them, "You have never read the Bible, have you?" "O, yes, and I believe every word in it is the word of God." Well, I believe that the Bible contains the word of God, and the words of good men and the words of bad men; the words of good angels and the words of bad angels and words of the devil.[9]

Recognizing that the scriptures are fallible—and that superficial readings are harmful—gives us liberty to approach the scriptures with caution and with a more questing spirit. There is good reason behind the injunction to *search* the scriptures (D&C 1:37). Maturing into the recognition that scriptures, like prophets, are fallible, creates a dilemma many have felt when we leave such golden calves behind: What is the benefit, then, of putting our faith in an imperfect voice? Our canonical scriptures clearly bear the imprint of God's inspiration, and we should treat them with reverence—even while recognizing that the Spirit is not the source of every word.

We do have at least one revealed litmus test for truth; it comes from the greatest of Joseph Smith's revelations, Moses 7. There we encounter the Weeping God of Enoch, the "Man of Holiness," and the Father of the "Son of Man" (Moses 7:35; 6:57). This magnificent epiphany provides us a template that corrects the greatest evil in the history of Christian theology—the God the Father who is divested of emotion, passion, vulnerability, and capacity to weep real tears in shared suffering with His children. C. S. Lewis did not know this scripture, but he did infer the great truth it taught. Writing to a friend, he acknowledged the danger of assuming that our own moral sensibility is the appropriate standard for judging God's actions. We run the risk of presentism, personal subjectivity, and finite perspective when we dismiss out of hand biblical depictions we find uncomfortable. "I see the grave danger we run by doing so," Lewis wrote. "But the dangers of believing in a God whom we cannot but regard as evil, and then, in mere terrified flattery calling Him 'good' and worshiping Him, is still greater danger. *The ultimate question is whether the doctrine of the goodness of God or that of the inerrancy of Scriptures is to prevail when they conflict.* We think the doctrine of the goodness of God is the more certain of the two" (emphasis added).[10]

Lewis was but repeating a maxim of John Wesley, the founder of Methodism, whom Brigham Young called "as good [a man] who ever walked the earth."[11] Wesley stated, "But you say you will prove it by the Scripture. Hold! What will you prove by Scripture? that God is worse than the devil? It cannot be. Whatever that scripture proves, it can never prove this; whatever its true meaning be, this cannot be its true meaning. . . . This I know, better it were to say it had no sense at all, than to say it had such a sense as this."[12] The best question we might ask ourselves is this: Does what I am reading expand my heart and mind, or does it harrow the mind and constrict the heart? (Alma 32:34).

Many early church fathers and mothers remained true and faithful to their understanding of the parental nature of God. Macrina (324–79 AD), the sister and teacher of the church father Gregory of Nyssa, taught that the godlike qualities of the soul draw it to those same qualities in the divine, "by means of the movement and the activity of love."[13] Later, the anchoress Julian of Norwich would declare that God is not capable of wrath because "wrath and friendship be two contraries."[14] What J. Reuben Clark said of spoken scripture must pertain equally well to that which is written: "I have given some thought to this question, and the answer thereto so far as I can determine, is: We can tell when the speakers [and writers] are 'moved upon by the Holy Ghost' only when we, ourselves, are 'moved upon by the Holy Ghost.' In a way, this completely shifts the responsibility from them to us to determine when they so speak."[15]

The call to discipleship is not for the faint of heart: "Then Jesus said to His disciples, If anyone [desires] to come after me, let him forget self and lose sight of his own interests, and let him pick up his cross and carry it, and let him [take] the same road with me that I travel" (Matt. 16:24, Wuest expanded translation). While the road Jesus traveled led to our exaltation, the work of discipleship is costly, painful, and grueling. Saints are good at service and at sacrifice. We live a high-demand faith, as sociologists recognize. We give up time, and money, and energy. However, we are not a people overly given to contemplation or to devotional prayer and pondering. In Oliver Cowdery's 1834 version of the Articles of Faith, he wrote, "We believe that God is the same in all ages; and that it requires the same holiness, purity, and religion, to save a man now, as it did anciently."[16] Unfortunately, that article was dropped from our canonized version. We Saints have typically been as industrious as bees. As Wilford Woodruff once said with some impatience, "Strangers and the Christian world marvel" at our emphasis on "temporal work," and responded that "we can't build up Zion sitting on a hemlock slab singing ourselves away to everlasting bliss; we have to cultivate the earth, to take the rocks and elements out of the mountains and rear Temples to the Most High God."[17] Spencer W. Kimball's favorite motto, to which he so often reverted, was "Do it!" As Terry Eagleton reminds us, the Gospel of Matthew teaches, "Eternity lies not in a grain of sand but in a glass of water. The cosmos revolves on comforting the sick."[18] In this essential sphere of active, engaged, service-oriented discipleship, Latter-day Saints have excelled.

We have not done as well in the meditative, contemplative half of discipleship. One reason may be our language of gospel "fulness," which seduces us into a kind of complacency. We have modern prophets, we have additional scripture, we have a correlated curriculum, and we believe we have answers to all those questions that haunt human history. We claim to know where we come from, why we are here, and where we are going. All of this adds up to a picture of completion, wholeness, satiety. If we are not smug, we are satisfied. We read a scripture that mocks the world for their self-satisfaction: "A Bible! A Bible! We have got a Bible, and there cannot be any more Bible" (2 Ne. 29:3). But do we liken that overconfident contentment to ourselves, as Nephi admonished? (1 Ne. 19:23).

Bearing the cross of discipleship involves the strenuous effort of the mind, as well as that of the body and the heart. B. H. Roberts encouraged discipleship that is more intellectually effortful:

> Mental laziness is the vice of men, especially with reference to divine things. Men seem to think that because inspiration and revelation are factors in connection with the things of God, therefore the pain and stress of mental effort are not required; that by some means these elements act somewhat as Elijah's ravens and feed us without effort on our part. . . . "Why then should man strive and trouble himself to understand? Much study is still a weariness of the flesh." So men reason; and just now it is much in fashion to laud "the simple faith;" which is content to believe without understanding, or even without much effort to understand.[19]

Joseph Smith reminded us that "The things of God are of deep import; and time, and experience, and careful and ponderous and solemn thoughts can only find them out. Thy mind, O man! if thou wilt lead a soul unto salvation, must stretch as high as the utmost heavens, and search into and contemplate the darkest abyss, and the broad expanse of eternity."[20]

Some of that stretching may require a more rigorous consideration of the language we employ to convey gospel understanding that is still unfolding as the Restoration proceeds apace. And we recognize that as more Latter-day Saint women's voices are incorporated into our discourse, that understanding is enriched and broadened.[21] Joseph also prophesied that "it shall come to pass in that day, that every man shall hear the fulness of the gospel in his own tongue, and in his own language" (D&C 90:11). That prophecy may be about something other than foreign tongues. The Lord said that commandments were given to us "in [our] weakness, after the manner of [our] language" (D&C 1:24). In section 19 of the Doctrine and Covenants, the Lord made clear that scriptural language does not always mean what we think it means; some wording is chosen deliberately "that it might work upon the hearts of the children of men" (verse 7). Brigham Young emphasized that language effective in one generation is not in another: "When God speaks to the people, he does it in a manner to suit their circumstances and capacities. . . . Should the Lord Almighty send an angel to re-write the Bible, it would in many places be very different from what it now is. And I will even venture to say that if the Book of Mormon were now to be re-written, in many instances it would materially differ from the present translation. According as people are willing to receive the things of God, so the heavens send forth their blessings."[22]

The "traditions of the fathers," embedded in an inherited religious language, continue to injure us. Language calculated to operate on nineteenth-century minds (and those of earlier epochs) may not be the most efficacious for *our* moment in history. The work of Restoration, to be complete, must include the casting off of those traditions, presuppositions, frameworks, paradigms, and vocabulary that still fill the garden of the gospel like tenacious weeds. The "plain and precious things" restored cannot attain their full splendor unless and until they are fully unencumbered by those traditions that still pervade our language and our conceptions alike. We need a new vocabulary, a new gospel grammar, freed from the corruptions of our Christian heritage.

The visionary member of the Seventy B. H. Roberts foresaw this need and hoped for its fulfillment in our day. He found his inspiration in the writings of the eminent American philosopher Josiah Royce. Disciples, Royce said, "are of two sorts. There are, first, the disciples pure and simple. . . . They expound, and defend, and ward off foes, and live and die faithful to one formula. . . . On the other hand, there are disciples of a second sort. . . . The seed that the sower strews upon [his] fields springs up in [his] soil, and bears fruit—thirty, sixty, an hundredfold. . . . Disciples of the second sort cooperate in the works of the Spirit . . . [and] help lead . . . to a *truer expression*" (our emphasis). B. H. Roberts read these words and built them into a prophecy and a call to action. "Mormonism," he said, "calls for [these disciples of the second sort,] disciples who will not be content with merely repeating some of its truths, but will develop its truths; and enlarge it by that development. . . . The disciples of 'Mormonism,' growing discontented with the necessarily primitive methods which have hitherto prevailed in sustaining the doctrine, . . . will cast them in new formulas; cooperating in the works of the Spirit, until they help to give to the truths received a more forceful expression."[23]

NOTES

1   Joseph Smith History 1:12.

2   Diarmaid MacCulloch, *The Reformation: A History* (New York: Viking, 2004), xxi.

3   See Adolf von Harnack's chapter "Marcion's Christianity in Light of Church History and the Philosophy of Religion," in *Marcion: The Gospel of the Alien God*, ed. Adolf von Harnack (Eugene, OR: Wipf and Stock, 1990), 133–45.

4   Hilarion Alfeyev, *The Spiritual World of Isaac the Syrian* (Collegeville, MN: Cistercian, 2000), 283–84.

5   Francine R. Bennion, "A Latter-day Saint Theology of Suffering," in *At the Pulpit*, ed. Jennifer Reeder and Kate Holbrook (Salt Lake City: Church Historian's Press, 2017), 219.

6   "The Chicago Statement on Biblical Inerrancy," *Themalios* 4, no. 3 (April 1979), https://www.thegospelcoalition.org/themelios/article/the-chicago-statement-on-biblical-inerrancy/.

7   Andrew F. Ehat and Lyndon W. Cook, ed., *The Words of Joseph Smith* (Orem, UT: Grandin Book Company, 1991), 211.

8   George Q. Cannon, "Discourse by Elder Geo. Q. Cannon, in *Journal of Discourses,* 21:10, 76.

9   Brigham Young, "Discourse by President Brigham Young," in *Journal of Discourses,* 18:175.

10   C. S. Lewis, *Collected Letters* (New York: HarperCollins, 2004), 3:1436–37.

11   Richard S. Van Wagoner, ed., *The Complete Discourses of Brigham Young* (Salt Lake City: Smith-Petit Foundation, 2009), 3:1480.

12   John Wesley, *Sermons on Several Occasions*, ed. Thomas Summers (Nashville: Stevenson & Owen, 1855), 4:384–85.

13   Morwenna Ludlow, *Universal Salvation: Eschatology in the Thought of Gregory of Nyssa and Karl Rahner* (New York: Oxford University Press, 2000), 61.

14   Denise N. Baker, ed. *The Showings of Julian of Norwich*, 14.49 (New York: Norton, 2005), 67. We have modernized the spelling and at times modified the translation.

15   J. Reuben Clark, "When Are Church Leaders' Words Entitled to Claim of Scripture?" *Church News*, July 31, 1954, 2.

16   Oliver Cowdery, "Address," *Messenger & Advocate* 1, no. 1 (October 1834): 2.

17   Wilford Woodruff, "Unchangeableness of the Gospel," in *Journal of Discourses*, 16:268.

18   Terry Eagleton, *The Meaning of Life: A Very Short Introduction* (New York: Oxford University Press, 2008), 95.

19   B. H. Roberts, *The Seventy's Course of Theology, Fifth Year* (Salt Lake City: The Deseret News, 1912), iv–v.

20   Joseph Smith, "History, 1838–1856, volume C-1, [2 November 1838–31 July 1842] [b]" p. 904b, The Joseph Smith Papers, accessed August 12, 2020, https://www.josephsmithpapers.org/paper-summary/history-1838 -1856-volume-c-1-2-november-1838-31-july-1842/86.

21   There are steps we can take to fill in the gaps. Eliza R. Snow's discourses are now published online by the Church Historian's Press, as is the extensive range of Latter-day Saint women's voices collected in *At the Pulpit*, edited by Jennifer Reeder and Kate Holbrook.

22   Young, *Complete Discourses*, 4:2033–34.

23   B. H. Roberts, "The Disciples of Mormonism," *Improvement Era*, July 1906, 712–13. He is citing Royce's introduction to *Fisk's Work*. Both are cited in Joseph Jeppson, "Notes and Comments," *Dialogue* 1, no. 4 (Winter 1966): 133–34.

PART TWO

Making All
Things New

CHAPTER FOUR

A New Language

Rewriting "Traditions of the Fathers"

*Does the decay of belief among educated people in
the West precede the decay of language used to define
and explore belief, or do we find the fire of belief
fading in us only because the words are sodden with
overuse and imprecision, and will not burn?*[1]

What we believe to be true of our deepest nature, and what
we believe to be true of God's nature, has real-world consequences. How we understand God, and the quality of Their
love, conditions our own ability to receive and reciprocate love.
Conceptions of human sin and worthiness profoundly impact
every relationship into which we enter. Confidence—or lack of
confidence—in the destiny toward which Heavenly Parents are
guiding us cannot help but determine our levels of joyfulness or
anxiety. How we understand words like *proving* and *testing* infuses
our lives with a sense of adventure or of dread, of beauty or of
scrupulosity. If we recognize the previously outlined revisions,
omissions, and intrusions into the Great Plan of Happiness to
be some of the "traditions of the fathers which are not correct,"
then how do these traditions continue to inform our lives as
aspiring disciples committed to a restored Church and gospel?

While we have not inherited the explicit claims those creeds articulate, we have inherited the vocabulary that was shaped in the Reformation and post-Reformation centuries. What one hears when the word *sin* is spoken, what we envision by the term *God*, or what it means to be *saved*, or *saved by grace*, has already been determined by centuries of usage. Reclaiming those terms for a new dispensation is an act of imaginative resistance.

The Restoration is a process, not an event, and it is still incomplete. We know this for a number of reasons. The Book of Mormon itself refers to that Nephite record as intended to recapture "much of my gospel" (1 Ne. 13:34). Doctrinal restoration is progressive. In 1895, after dramatic changes to the nature of temple sealing (by family rather than into prophetic dynasties), Elder Marriner Merrill said, "Perhaps the Lord has not revealed everything to [the presidency of the Church] yet, but He will reveal line upon line, as He did to the Prophet over a year ago. . . . So other things may be revealed by and by."[2] Five years later, Lorenzo Snow remarked that "seventy years ago this Church was organized with six members. We commenced, so to speak, as an infant. We had our prejudices to combat. Our ignorance troubled us in regard to what the Lord intended to do and what He wanted us to do. . . . We advanced to boyhood, and still we undoubtedly made some mistakes, which . . . generally arise from a . . . lack of experience, . . . we have not yet arrived at perfection. There are many things for us to do yet."[3] In our own day, President Nelson has reaffirmed Restoration as a work in progress.[4] Part of that ongoing work may be reshaping our vocabulary to more fully and accurately reflect Joseph's revelatory insights.

In such a spirit, we offer here what we hope may provide bases for an ongoing conversation about the language of the Restoration. I (Terryl) realized many years ago that when an evangelical asked if I had been saved, we weren't even speaking the same language. What do Latter-day Saints mean by salvation? Asking what we believe we are being saved from and for entails a reconsideration of the Fall, heaven, and sin. Sin presumes the necessity of repentance and the possibility of forgiveness, which is predicated on the Atonement of Jesus Christ. If we understand salvation and Atonement in fresh ways, then grace will have a different complexion as well. A theory of grace conditions our definitions of obedience and worthiness, so those terms will need reexamination. In Christian thought, the entirety of the story generally ends at judgment. Since the Saints espouse a different story with a different beginning and end, our conception of judgment shifts accordingly.

Here are a few caveats about what this sketch is and is not: We are neither offering dogmatic definitions nor offering a comprehensive treatment. We are trying to model and inspire fresh ways of thinking through the religious vocabulary that pervades our wounded world and particularly our Church that is still emerging from the wilderness. Language bears within itself the power to hurt or to heal, to obfuscate or to clarify, to instill with despair or to expand with hope. As Robert MacFarlane taught us, "Language is fundamental to the possibility of re-wonderment, for language does not just register experience, it produces it" (our emphasis).[5] Our language shapes our mind and heart, our Church culture, our world. Our religious language conditions all of our experience and negates or makes possible our encounter with what is most holy. These tentative efforts in the direction of a new vocabulary worthy of a God-given dispensation in which all things are made new are intended to prompt healing, clarity, and hope.

NOTES

1   Christian Wiman, *My Bright Abyss* (New York: Farrar, Straus and Giroux, 2014), 124.

2   Marriner W. Merrill, "Temple Work," in *The Deseret Weekly* (Salt Lake City: Deseret News, 1895), 51:610.

3   Lorenzo Snow, "First Day," in *Seventieth Annual Conference of the Church of Jesus Christ of Latter-day Saints* (Salt Lake City: Deseret News, 1900), 1.

4   See Dallin H. Oaks, "The Great Plan of Happiness," *Ensign* 23, no. 11 (November 1993): 72–75.

5   Robert MacFarlane, *Landmarks* (New York: Penguin, 2015), 25.

CHAPTER FIVE

Salvation

From Rescue to Realization

Only in Restoration scripture do we learn the backstory and the unfathomable ambition behind Jesus's words to His disciples, whom He envisioned as friends and peers (John 15:15). That backstory is as follows: In a large assembly surrounded by fellow spirits, our Heavenly Parents invited us into more intimate and equal communion with Themselves. Generous to overflowing, desirous of helping us grow into beings fully capable of "the abundant life," an Eternal Father and His Divine Companion undertook to parent us to the point that we can share in Their condition. Because of God's "spiritual thirst," as Julian the God-touched mystic perceived, God "longeth ever to bring us to the fulness of joy."[1] The parenting process, boiled down to its purest, simplest essence, was for our Heavenly Parents to school us in the kind of love that filled and motivated Themselves—absolute love. "At the end of this process," Chieko Okazaki wrote, "our Heavenly Parents will have sons and daughters who are their peers, their friends and their colleagues."[2]

We understand, in a way that is radically distinct from Christian conceptions, that salvation is the flowering of a divine potential, not the correction of an innate fault. The path by which we come to experience heaven will be shaped accordingly. What the previous discussion places at the center of any conception of salvation is the quickening power of authentic relationships. We might venture a definition of *salvation*: to be *saved* is to become the kind of persons, in the kinds of relationships, that constitute the divine nature.

The *becoming* is the key term here. This understanding of *saved* was taught in the School of the Prophets:

> Let us ask, where shall we find a prototype into whose likeness we may be assimilated, in order that we may be made partakers of life and salvation? Or in other words, where shall we find a saved being? For if we can find a saved being, we may ascertain, without much difficulty, what all others must be, in order to be saved—they must be like that individual or they cannot be saved. . . . Whatever constitutes the salvation of one, will constitute the salvation of every creature which will be saved. . . . We ask, then, where is the prototype? or where is the saved being? We conclude as to the answer of this question . . . it is Christ: all will agree in this that he is the prototype or standard of salvation, or in other words, that he is a saved being. . . . How is it that he is saved? . . . Because he is a just and holy being; and if he were anything different from what he is he would not be saved; for his salvation depends on his being precisely what he is and nothing else. . . . Thus says John, in his first epistle, Behold, now we are the sons of God, and it doth not appear what we shall be; but we know, that when he shall appear we shall be like him; for we shall see him as he is.[3]

Several remarkable facts follow from this definition of a saved being. To be saved does not mean to be rescued, redeemed, or otherwise restored from a position of deficit. This position of deficit is where we too often get off on the wrong foot, unconsciously buying into a framework that is the universal Christian default with which the story begins (see chapter 7, "Fall," and chapter 9, "Sin"). Our story, the greatest cosmic adventure of all time, starts in heaven with the prospect of salvation—which Joseph renames exaltation. Exaltation, eternal life, theosis: this is the ambitious project of god-like growth, addition, education, becoming, and transformation.

This metamorphosis is the most important feature of Latter-day Saint salvation. The process is not recuperative. It is not a response to a past catastrophe; it is the realization of a future possibility. It is additive, not restorative. The explicit focus of salvation is on what one can be, not what one must say or do. The language of becoming "a just and holy being," as we will see, has profound consequences on the meaning of grace. This is why we emphasized that fatal moment in the Reformation when Luther reinvented salvation as the "declaring" rather than the "becoming" righteous or holy. With Luther, salvation became something that God can give us—a gift He grants or withholds at His whim—on His preconditions. As Saints, many of us still relate to God on that false assumption; we live with the constant fear that we are failing to please him, to measure up, as if He is looking for reasons to deny us the winner's cup. We lose sight of the fact that God is running the race with us, not waiting at the finish line to declare us victor or loser. Neither is "our universe . . . a despotic monarchy, with God above the starry canopy and ourselves down here; it is a spiritual commonwealth with God in the midst of us."[4]

Restoration theology is, from the first word, far more ambitious, presumptuous, and gloriously aspirational than we may recognize. Restoration theology goes far beyond the current Christian hope of personal redemption from death and hell. Our faith tradition aspires to make us into the likeness of our Heavenly Parents. Our sin, as Saints, may be in thinking that such an endeavor could be anything other than wrenching, costly, inconceivably difficult, and at times unimaginably painful. We do not become, in C. S. Lewis's phrase, "little Christs"[5] by a couple of well-spent hours ministering to our assigned families and abstaining from tea and coffee. The focusing lenses of our religion—its scriptural promises, its temple rituals, its discipline of prayer, and its priesthood piercings of the veil—bring us into closer contact with the divine, even if that participation in that divine nature is still a long way off. We are still very much in the morning of an eternity of striving, and our theology is commensurately ambitious, open-ended, and dauntingly generative of unexplored ramifications.

NOTES

1   Denise N. Baker, ed., *The Showings of Julian of Norwich*, 13.40, (New York: Norton, 2005), 55. We have modernized the spelling and at times modified the translation.

2   Chieko N. Okazaki, *Sanctuary* (Salt Lake City: Deseret Book, 1997), 59.

3   1 John 3:2–3; *Theology Lecture Seventh*, 1835 D&C, pp. 66–67.

4   Walter Rauschenbusch, *A Theology for the Social Gospel* (New York: Abingdon Press, 1917), 174. Cited in Joanne Carlson Brown and Cariole R. Bone, ed., *Christianity, Patriarchy, and Abuse: A Feminist Critique* (New York: Pilgrim Press, 1989), 8.

5   C. S. Lewis, *Mere Christianity* (New York: Simon & Schuster Touchstone, 1996), 171.

Heaven

From "Where" to "with Whom"

S ome Christians may say that their story also begins in heaven—
in a paradisiacal garden before sin entered the world. However,
this heaven is not the same as the one we know as Latter-day
Saints. We understand, of course, that in the first place, only
Eve and Adam were in that paradisiacal locale and station. And
in the second, an eternal stasis devoid of knowledge or striving
or posterity does not sound like a condition most of us would
choose. On the contrary, Lehi found the garden state more of a
horror to contemplate than a heaven. Without the experience of
opposites, he says, "righteousness could not be brought to pass,
neither wickedness, neither holiness nor misery, neither good nor
bad. Wherefore, all things must needs be a compound in one;
wherefore, . . . it must needs remain as dead. . . . Wherefore, [the
earth] must needs have been created for a thing of naught; wherefore there would have been no purpose in the end of its creation"
(2 Ne. 2:11–12). How utterly incredible that, for Lehi, the fate
worse than death was perpetual stasis. Sarah Kimball was perhaps
the first Latter-day Saint to affirm Lehi's reconceiving of this re-
puted paradise as "the dark valley of ignorance and stagnation."[1]

Although the Latter-day Saint belief in the possibility of
theosis, deification, and God-becoming is almost dauntingly
presumptuous, our corresponding conception of heaven is sur-

prisingly modest: "that same sociality which exists among us here
. . . coupled with eternal glory," revealed Joseph (D&C 130:2). If
salvation is about what we are to become as individuals, heaven
is the name given to those relationships in which individuals find
fulness of joy. That may not be a complicated idea, but its implications are far-reaching. For one thing, it clarifies why neither
salvation nor heaven are rewards that God can dispense, or that
we can earn. Relationships are forged. Life is the school of love,
and our growing capacity for love constitutes the bricks out of
which the heavenly Zion will be constructed. The original spirit of
Christ's message was evident in the hope of the sixteenth-century
nonconformist Katharina Schütz: "I seek nothing other than that
we may be saved together with each other."[2] Or as the great British poet, John Milton, noted of the Creation story, "Loneliness
is the first thing which God's eye named not good."[3] Heaven is
relationship.

A cardinal Christian doctrine is that of humans as pilgrims:
"Man, as long as he exists in this world, is characterized by an
inward, as it were ontological quality of being on-the-way to
somewhere else."[4] This is a beautiful conception, one that we feel
and gladly embrace. However, one scholar notes that in traditional Christianity, "the strongly held doctrine is that the state
of pilgrimage, the status viatoris, ends at death."[5] By emphatic
contrast, Brigham Young stipulated, "When we have learned
to live according to the full value of the life we now possess,
we are prepared for further advancement in the scale of eternal
progression—for a more glorious and exalted sphere."[6] Heaven
is process.

It may be that God knows the future, as They know the
past, because They know all things. It is also possible that, as some
religious thinkers both within and outside our tradition have held,
the future does not yet exist. Hence the future is not one of those
"all things" that can be objects of knowledge. However, we do

know that God's knowledge is complete and therefore sufficient for us to repose confidence in Their plans and purposes. There is a different kind of comfort in believing that as long as free will exists, we will continue to act and choose and create in ways that are never fully predictable and that the eternities can unfold before us, as our relationships do, in ways that can delight and surprise us—and perhaps God as well.

NOTES

1 S. M. K. [Sarah M. Kimball], "Plea for the Women of Massachusetts and Mother Eve, vs. Kate Bowers," *Woman's Exponent* 2, no.18 (February 15, 1874): 141. Cited in Boyd J. Petersen, "'Redeemed from the Curse Place Upon Her': Dialogic Discourse on Eve in the *Women's Exponent*," *Journal of Mormon History* 40, no. 1 (Winter 2014): 155–56.

2 Diana Butler Bass, *A People's History of Christianity* (New York: HarperCollins, 1989), 168.

3 Cited in Stephen Greenblatt, *The Rise and Fall of Adam and Eve* (New York: Norton, 2017), 179.

4 Josef Pieper, *Death and Immortality* (South Bend, IN: St. Augustine's Press, 2000), 75–76.

5 Carl Cranney, *The Final Answer to God: The Fate of the Unevangelized in Catholic and Latter-day Saint Thought* (PhD diss., Catholic University of America, 2020), 48.

6 Brigham Young, "Necessity of Paying Due Attention to Temporal Duties," in *Journal of Discourses,* 9:168.

CHAPTER SEVEN

Fall

From Corruption to Ascension

No clearer distinction could be made between the Latter-day Saint conception of human life and that of fellow Christians than is suggested by the entirely typical statement of E. Brooks Holifield: "The drama of salvation began when the Father and Son agreed to redeem the creation from the effects of the fall."[1] Another representative Christian authority refers to the parameters of the Christian story as "the whole complex of the Divine dispensation from the fall of Adam to the Redemption through Christ."[2] These brief formulations have an astounding implication: the entirety of the Christian message is reducible to a tragedy rectified. A third mainstream writer affirms this premise: "God's purpose and goal in redemption is to reverse the sin, corruption and death introduced into humanity by Adam."[3] Or, in the words of the greatest contemporary scholar of the Reformation, "Jesus . . . died in Palestine for human sin in order to retrieve something from the wreckage of humanity's failure."[4]

As Latter-day Saints we sense neither wreckage nor failure in the events of Eden. On one occasion, Joseph Smith said he was frequently asked, "Do you believe the Bible?" His reply was, "If we do, we are the only people under heaven that does. For there are none of the religious sects of the day that do."[5] His answer was hyperbolic but entirely accurate with regard to Genesis 3:22:

"And the Lord God said, Behold, the man is become as one of us."
Without exception, legions of commentators throughout Christian history have refused to take those words at face value. "God was mocking Adam," explained the fourth-century theologian Ephrem the Syrian.[6] His contemporary John Chrysostom went further and simply denied the accuracy of the passage, since it is obvious, he wrote, that "they did not become god" or "receive the knowledge of good and evil."[7] Centuries later, Andrew Willet, a commentator on Genesis, insisted that the Lord was "speak[ing] ironically." Reformers Phillip Melanchton, Peter Vermigli, and Konrad Pellikan all also employed the term *irony* to explain away the plain meaning of Genesis 3:22.[8]

Joseph Smith, by contrast, read the verse as a simple statement of fact. And we note that neither the word *sin* nor *Fall* occurs in the sacred narrative. The Great Plan conceived in the heavenly assembly anticipated Eve's decision as the necessary prelude to the transition of the entire human family from premortality into mortality: "God foreordained the fall."[9] In Joseph Smith's mouth, the Fall is no tragic descent. It is fruitful *ascent*. "[Human beings] were *born* into the world by the fall," is how Joseph characterizes the aftermath in his first revision of the account in Genesis.[10]

This understanding was evident in the early Church before Augustine rewrote the narrative. In the second century, the first authority to expound the story of the garden was Irenaeus. "For him," writes one scholar, "man's role is not that of one created perfect only to fall into sin but of one brought into being with all the imperfections endemic in human nature but with the prospect of development as a part of God's creative plan into the divine likeness revealed to him in Jesus. The emphasis here is not on a Fall in the past but upon a growth in the future."[11] Notice how exactly this statement agrees with what we stated previously, that the essence of the original gospel story was centered in Christ's invitation to follow in His steps. And Christians like Irenaeus saw what happened in Eden as part of that process.

Latter-day Saints reject the entire story of "salvation" as reconstituted by Augustine and his descendants.[12] Sadly, we still find ourselves employing a term—*the Fall*—whose general meaning we emphatically reject—presumably because the term is so universally understood that we are forced to use it as part of a Christian common language. As children of the Restoration, however, we would be well-served always to put "Fall" in quotation marks.

In the Genesis account, Eve and Adam are blessed to "be fruitful and multiply." In Joseph's translation of the book of Abraham, there is a slight but momentous change: "And the Gods said: We will bless them. And the Gods said: *We will cause them* to be fruitful and multiply" (4:28; our emphasis). The Gods are the active agents behind the couple's fecundity. Clarifying that this capacity to conceive is the specific form that Eve and Adam's "blessing" takes adds weight to Their intention that Eve should eat the fruit and thereby launch the project of human life. Her appellation, the Mother of All Living, bears comparison with the only other two women who are generative of so much light and life: Heavenly Mother and Mary, the mother of the Lord.

Relief Society president Sarah Kimball's assessment of Eve deserves canonization: "Our great maternal progenitor is entitled to reverent honor for braving the peril that brought earth's children from the dark valley of ignorance and stagnation, and placed them on the broad, progressive plain, where they, knowing good and evil, joy and sorrow, may become Gods. . . . Mother Eve, for taking the initiative in this advance movement, should receive encomiums of praise."[13]

Ancient and modern scripture alike affirm Eve's righteous motivation in seeking a fruit that was "desirable to make one wise" (Gen. 3:6). In fact, the book of Enoch designates the tree from which she partook as "the Tree of Wisdom from which [Enoch's] old father and aged mother . . . ate and came to know wisdom; and their eyes were opened."[14] When young Solomon prays for wisdom at the beginning of his kingship—a prayer that pleases God—he asks for a heart that can "discern between good and evil," the same gift the tree in Eden offered (1 Kgs. 3:9). The Bible admonishes us to "get wisdom" (Prov. 4:5), and it was Joseph's explicit pursuit of this wisdom, encouraged by James, that launched the Restoration. It should not surprise us, then, that the first canonized commandment of the new dispensation before the Church was even organized was an injunction to follow Eve's example: "Seek . . . for wisdom, and behold, the mysteries of God shall be unfolded unto you, and then shall you be made rich. Behold, he that has eternal life is rich" (D&C 6:7, given in April 1829; the command was repeated in D&C 11:7). This wisdom Eve sought is the basis of eternal life.

And yet, clearly, *something* tragic happened with the mortal transformations ushered in by the choice of Eve and Adam, and this consequence demands attention. First and foremost, death entered human experience. As Saints, we may often pass right over the greatest destroyer of human happiness, the source of universal angst and the primal catalyst behind all religious questing—the specter of death—as if it were a mere blip on the screen of existence. At least, those secure in their faith may envision the process as a seamless transition, loved ones bidding us farewell and loved ones from beyond shepherding us across the threshold of death, with never a pause in the valley of death itself. In our minds, the rescue may be so complete, so assured, so fact-of-the-future, that we may never suffer the pangs of incertitude that others do—the agony of anticipated absence that is permanent. Such blithe faith can come at a cost; perhaps only a chasm of fear and helplessness before the brute fact of death can accommodate the flood of grace that fills us with new life.

Jacob marvels at the gift of a universal resurrection, breaking into ecstatic praise: "O the wisdom of God, His mercy and grace! . . . Because of the way of deliverance of our God, the Holy One of Israel, this death, of which I have spoken, which is the temporal, shall deliver up its dead; which death is the grave. Wherefore, death and hell must deliver up their dead, . . . and it is by the power of the resurrection of the Holy One of Israel. . . . O how great the plan of our God!" (2 Ne. 9:8–13). In *that* sense of a susceptibility to physical dissolution, Eve and Adam and their posterity fell. And in *that* sense they and we need redemption and rescue. In this regard, the Book of Mormon provides a powerful reorientation of the meaning of that redemption. For most Christians, the word *redemption* conjures up rescue from sin, Satan, and hell. The "purpose of redemption," as we quoted one scholar previously, was primarily to "reverse" sin and corruption. As we will see, the very word *redemption* led to peculiar notions among some early Christians of Christ serving as "bait" in order to "ransom" us from the devil. For Book of Mormon prophets, Christ's role as Redeemer is focused on His gift of resurrection. Alma pairs "resurrection of the dead" and "redemption" (Mosiah 18:1–2); Lehi taught that the principal purpose of Christ's sacrifice was "to bring to pass the resurrection of the dead" (2 Ne. 2:8); Nephi, too, believed His sufferings were "that the resurrection might pass upon all men" (2 Ne. 9:21–22).

This gift of resurrection, universal and unearned, is an unconditional promise that we will live again. Such a supernal gift is largely obscured in the history of Christian conflict, consumed with doctrinal disputes over secondary concerns. The wars of the Reformation era and the fires of the Inquisition were fueled by disputes over the nature of the Trinity, the degree of God's presence in the Eucharist, the question of whether sacraments are symbols or channels of grace, and so forth. In our lives, we too may so anguish over the minutiae of worship forms or issues of little import that we forget the most unfathomably remarkable gift of all. As one Latter-day Saint with more hope than certainty wrote, "It seems a pity to take one's immortality for granted, to expect it and count on it. It seems a pity to be so sheltered from the terror of death that one's gratitude for the resurrection is merely dutiful and perfunctory. Perhaps truly there are religious advantages to doubt. Perhaps only a doubter can appreciate the miracle of life without end."[15]

As Eve and Adam's posterity, we fall in a second way. Acquiring at conception our individual "coat of skins" (which some early Christians thought was a metaphor for our spirits' embodiment), we become biological organisms, inheriting all of those instincts, appetites and tendencies toward self-preservation with which nature endowed us. The theological step of incalculable damage was to associate those features of our new identities with sin and guilt and to make such sin and guilt the central facts of the human condition. In other words, it is the action of our natural Darwinian selves that can impel us in a direction contrary to God and godliness. It is *that* side of our nature, that which comes to us *through* nature, that if unchecked can become the "enemy to God," not our innate self which is "whole from the foundation of the world" (Mosiah 16:5; Moses 6:54).

Christian handbooks declare that the cause and substance of that Fall was sin, and sin is equated with disobedience—an affront to God, a form of rebellion against an absolute, perfect sovereign. Sin is "purposeful disobedience . . . to the known will of God," according to one authoritative source.[16] Catholic teaching about the New Testament sees sin as "above all" an offense "against God."[17] Given this near universal association of sin with disobedience, perhaps it would make sense to next examine the principle of obedience and sin in light of Restoration teachings.

NOTES

1   E. Brooks Holifield, *Theology in America* (New Haven: Yale University Press, 2003), 36.

2   "Theology," in *Oxford Dictionary of the Christian Church*, ed. F. L. Cross and E. A. Livingstone (Oxford: Oxford University Press, 2005), 1616.

3   Roger E. Olson, *The Story of Christian Theology* (Downers Grove, IL: InterVarsity Press, 1999), 277.

4   Diarmaid MacCulloch, *The Reformation: A History* (New York: Viking, 2004), 7.

5   "Elders' Journal, July 1838," p. 42, The Joseph Smith Papers, accessed April 28, 2020, https://www.josephsmithpapers.org/paper-summary/elders-journal-july-1838/10.

6   Andrew Louth, ed., *Ancient Christian Commentary on Scripture: Genesis 1–11* (Downers Grove, IL: InterVarsity, 2001), 1:100.

7   Chrysostom, "Homilies on Genesis 7," in Louth, *Ancient Christian Commentary,* 1:101.

8   John L. Thompson, ed., *Reformation Commentary on Scripture: Genesis 1–11* (Downers Grove, IL: InterVarsity, 2012), 1:177.

9   Andrew F. Ehat and Lyndon W. Cook, ed., *The Words of Joseph Smith* (Orem, UT: Grandin Book Company, 1991), 33.

10   Scott H. Faulring, Kent P. Jackson, and Robert J. Matthews, eds., Moses 6:59 in *Joseph Smith's New Translation of the Bible: Original Manuscripts* (Provo, UT: Religious Studies Center, 2004), 102. The 1878 and subsequent editions of the Pearl of Great Price, following the manuscript OT2, vary slightly: "By reason of transgression cometh the fall, which fall bringeth death." See Robert J. Matthews, "How We Got the Book of Moses," *Ensign* 26, no. 1 (January 1986): 46.

11   B. R. Rees, *Life*, in *Pelagius: Life and Letters* (Woodbridge, UK: Boydell, 1991), 57.

12   Augustine did not invent the doctrine out of a vacuum. Seeds have been traced to Egypt and even earlier, but Augustine gave it full form and enduring status. See Rees, *Pelagius*, 58–59.

13   Cited in Boyd Petersen, "Redeemed from the Curse Placed Upon Her: Dialogic Discourse on Eve in the Women's *Exponent*," *Journal of Mormon History* 40, no. 1 (2014): 155–56.

14   James H. Charlesworth, ed., "Enoch 1:32.6," in *Old Testament Pseudepigrapha* (Garden City: Doubleday, 1983), 1:28.

15   Levi S. Peterson, "A Christian by Yearning," in *The Wilderness of Faith*, ed. John Sillito (Salt Lake City: Signature, 1991), 134.

16   F. L. Cross and E. A. Livingstone, eds., "Sin," in *Oxford Dictionary of the Christian Church* (Oxford: Oxford University Press, 1997), 1505.

17   J. Lachowski, "Sin in the New Testament," in *New Catholic Encyclopedia*, 2nd. edition (Gale: Catholic University of America, 2003), 145.

CHAPTER EIGHT

Obedience

From Subject to Heir

I n the new framework of the Restoration, how do we understand obedience? We can begin with one paradigm-bursting
question that has lain scripturally embedded and seemingly
unnoticed for centuries—waiting to detonate with the power to
rewrite the nature of God's parenthood and our relationship to
Divine Parents. The scriptural setting is the story of Job and his
bewilderment in the face of what seems to him a suffering that is
clearly unmerited. In some ways, the story is reminiscent of Adam
and Eve in the garden because it revolves around a condition of
cognitive dissonance. In the Genesis story, Adam and Eve are told
to replenish the earth, but they are warned away from the only
means of replenishment: the tree of knowledge.[1] This is an apt
situation, if the purpose of this founding myth is to teach us what
is at the heart of the human condition: the difficult and generally
painful need to choose among competing values and competing
versions of the Good. (Even our Divine Parents are not exempt
from such anguished dilemmas, as when Their respect for our
agency competes with Their desire to spare us pain).

Job finds himself suffering his own kind of cognitive
dissonance, competing truths he cannot reconcile. God is just,
but Job is suffering unjustly. The root of his problem, as Elihu
will at last explain, is Job's deficient understanding of God,

the commandments, and the nature of sin and obedience. Like so many Christians of a thousand years hence, Job assumes that the point of obedience is to satisfy an arbitrary ruler who punishes any breach of His law. Job's friends confirm him in this view. "Who ever perished, being innocent?" asks Eliphaz (4:7). Job cannot locate any evil in his conduct, but Bildad objects: "Doth God pervert judgment? Or doth the Almighty pervert justice? (8:3). But "thou knowest I am not wicked," Job counters (10:7).

Without dissent, his companions insist that Job is deceived. If man is righteous, God is pleased, and as a just God He will bless him. If man sins, God is angry and will punish. The entire paradigm framing the dispute shifts seismically with the question asked by the newcomer Elihu. He appears like a wandering prophet to at last intercede, and with his question cuts through the common currency of sin and obedience and rocks the foundations of this theological paradigm. To Job and his earnest but erroneous friends, Elihu declares, "I would like to reply to you. . . . If you sin, how does that affect *him*? If your sins are many, what does that do to *him*? If you are righteous, what do you give *to him*, or what does *he receive* from your hand?" (35:4–7, New International Version; our emphases).

The implications of Elihu's rhetorical questions are astonishing, disconcerting, and, initially, beyond our ability to absorb. He is deconstructing any idea we (or Job and his companions) might have of God as a sovereign ruler. Our sins do not diminish God. They do not detract from God's majesty or divinity. Neither does our obedience enhance God's glory. Our actions, be they evil or righteous, *have no necessary, intrinsic bearing* on God. This knowledge is to turn the universe upside down. The whole language of God as sovereign, a deity who must be appeased, a jealous God whom we fear to offend—from ancient cultures through Hebraic conceptions to the present day—has infiltrated our sense of what it means to worship, to fear, to obey. Elihu's rhetorical question calls all such conceptions into doubt.

A subject who defies his king threatens the king's sovereignty. A vassal who disrespects his ruler undermines the ruler's authority and offends his liege lord. Judgment and punishment must follow. This is the unmistakable, but perverse, way in which Christianity has long taught of God, sin, and obedience. One preacher of this school proclaims, "It should be noted that in any repentance and returning to God there has to include a real sense of personal offense towards God. Sin is slapping the face of God! . . . When we commit a sin, it is primarily a sin against God! The essence is in reality a deep awareness of how much we have hurt God!"[2]

Clearly, in some sense, God *does* care about our choices for good or ill. Clearly, in some sense, God *does* respond to those choices. What Elihu is calling into question is the *why* behind God's response. Elihu is suggesting that God's relationship to us is not one predicated on obligation or sovereignty. God does not *owe* us blessings when we obey, and God's station does not *require* punishment when we disobey. If this suggestion is true, then epithets like *sovereign*, *ruler*, and *king* are not the most apt names for God's role and relationship to us. Therefore, obedience—its meanings and motives—might have an entirely different quality, as might forgiveness.

If we think of our God as Parent and explore the simple ramifications of a more literal application of that title, all the connotations of *obedience* shift. Elihu had suggested that perhaps our relationship to the divine is *not* transactional. We do not obey *in order* to secure blessings. God does not enjoin obedience *because* it affirms God's sovereignty. God does not bless us *because* we have earned the blessing. If these claims are true, then Heavenly Parents do not urge our repentance to assuage *Their* injury. In the medieval church, the sinner had to give "satisfaction" to be forgiven—"to compensate for the injury he had done to God."[3]

Clearly, in this view, God's only concern is for his *own* glory, not *our* welfare. Such a God would be the Supreme Narcissist.

It is unclear if Elihu believes that God is simply too remote, too transcendent, or too removed from human concerns to be bribed or offended by mortal actions or if he understands, as we should, that God's concern is a *chosen*, a *willed*, a *gifted* concern. The reality is that in our most loving relationships, we are injured because our love makes us vulnerable to injury. That is the truth about God's love. But only the parental nature of such love makes this clear: If my child disobeys my counsel, I am not (or not properly) angry. I do not react to protect my parental dignity; I am not jealous for my parental prerogatives; I am not concerned for my parental authority, or honor, or standing. I am saddened because in ignoring the counsel borne of my love and wisdom, my child opens herself to harm, to pain, to disappointment. I do not stand ready to reward the child for obedience or to punish for disobedience; her decision to follow the counsel redounds to her good, and disobedience to her harm. This, however, is the key fact: our relationship is not based in reciprocity. It cannot be, for the parent loves the child before the child is even cognizant of having a parent ("He first loved us" [1 Jn. 4:19].). And the child's affection for the parent becomes worthy of the name *love* only when it flows freely, independent of fear on the one hand and self-interest on the other.

When Elihu queries, "What harm does your sin do to God, or what benefit does he derive from your obedience?" we must not take this to mean that our Heavenly Parents are indifferent to our sin or virtue; rather, Their concern is a consequence of their freely given love and expresses the vulnerability that all love brings in its own wake. God does not *owe* us blessings or gratitude, and does not *insist* on punishment or retribution. God *experiences* joy in our growth and prosperity, and They *experience* sorrow in our missteps and the pain that follows, because They choose to love us.

There is no one-to-one relationship between our actions and our blessedness or suffering. As another prophet will write, and Jesus will affirm, the sun shines and the rain falls equally on those perceived to be good and on those perceived to be wicked (Job 2:10; Matt. 5:45). Obedience drawn out of us from fear is but slavery. Motivated by blessings, it is but economic calculation. We and Job are being taught that the motive for obedience must be love; and good parents, be they eternal or earthly, ask obedience for *our* benefit, not for their own. And if that is true, then the point of obedience is not that it is a litmus test of our servitude. Submission or rebellion is not the primary concern of an earthly parent whose interest lies in the well-being of the child. The problem with ignoring God's love-based counsel is that it short-circuits God's purpose behind those counsels—the growth in blessedness of the disciple. The early Christian Pelagius gave inspired advice: that we should think of obedience as a response to loving counsel rather than to divine command. He said, "Consider then, I beg you, the great difference between counsel and command: . . . the former invites you to do something, the latter threatens you if you fail to do it."[4]

Instances of this understanding erupt occasionally, with unexpected tenderness, even in the Old Testament text: "That thou mayest love the Lord thy God, and that thou mayest obey His voice, and that thou mayest cleave unto him: for he is thy life" (Deut. 30:20).

NOTES

1   Joseph's revision of the Bible intimated that it was no prohibition but a warning: "Nevertheless, thou mayest choose for thyself, for it is given unto thee" (Moses 3:17).

2   Robert A. Hanson, *Who Is in Control* (Maitland, FL: Xulon Press, 2012), 64. Cited in Josh Davis, "Confess Them and Forsake Them" (unpublished manuscript, December 2019).

3   Michael Massing, *Fatal Discord: Erasmus, Luther, and the Fight for the Western Mind* (New York: HarperCollins, 2018), 52.

4   Pelagius, "To Demetrias," in B. R. Rees, *Letters*, in *Pelagius: Life and Letters* (Woodbridge, UK: Boydell, 1991), 47.

CHAPTER NINE

Sin

From Guilt to Woundedness

The Augustinian revolution of the fourth century "would leave the Church in the West dominated by sin for centuries to come."[1] Augustine thought Paul's whole preoccupation was with sin, but as recent scholars have increasingly come to recognize, Paul's lament was a response to "his weakness. . . . Paul never felt guilt in the face of this weakness—pain yes, but not guilt."[2] Nevertheless, Christianity became refashioned around the dominant edifice of sin, and the whole framework of sin and salvation has for centuries been rooted in a paradigm of criminality. If we do not understand that, we will never come to recognize how that deeply rooted idea of criminality still colors our understanding not only of sin but also of judgment, guilt, and retribution. And that mistaken view operates in total disregard for the larger context in which sin operates—which context is the purpose behind our mortal journey.

Dame Julian of Norwich moved the discussion in this direction when she asked the question, Why is there sin? Why didn't God create a more perfect world, and us with more perfect character? "Sin is behovely," the Lord told her.[3] Needful. Fruitful. Productive of good. Clearly, sin cannot mean what we have taken it to mean, if Julian is correct. To call it "behovely" sounds counter to everything we have ever thought about sin. We have

seen it as an evil, vile, corrupt action following from a corrupt
nature. We find a very different explanation of sin in the book
of Moses—and a confirmation of Julian's astonishing claim that
what we call "sin" is something other than what we believed it to
be. Sin is indeed something that is "behovely."

Enoch relates how the Lord himself had explained to Eve
and Adam the meaning of what had transpired in the garden. He
validates Eve's insight that her decision was commendable, not
damnable. In Enoch's words, because of the couple's decision,
"we[, the human family,] are." Her gesture opened the conduit
for our ascent from premortality into this world. As a result,
Enoch notes, "we are made partakers of misery and woe" (Moses
6:48). Misery and woe, but not sin and guilt. The distinction
is crucial. As the Lord explains, "children . . . are whole from
the foundation of the world" (verse 54). And yet, in surprising
language, he then continues in what seems to be an Augustinian
vein: "children are conceived in sin" and as "they begin to grow
up, sin conceiveth in their hearts" (verse 55). This is understand-
ably confusing. If children are "conceived in sin" but are at the
same time "whole," then sin is not here referring to our personal
condition of culpability. And in fact, the Lord gives us new terms
in place of sin. We are born into a world of "misery and woe." We
are immersed in, confronted by, "the *bitter*, that [we] may know
to prize the good"—that is, the sweet (verse 55). "That we may
know" captures the educative, "behovely" nature of sin. "If not
for our transgression," if not for this experience of the bitter, Eve
confirms, we never should have known (experienced) good and
evil, and the joy of our redemption" (Moses 5:11).

Where an instructive *bitterness* is one way of viewing "sin" in
the book of Moses, the most pervasive image the New Testament
and Book of Mormon employ in reference to our condition is
woundedness. The angel uses that word to describe the human
condition to Nephi. When Nephi sees the Christ in vision, he

sees Him *not* preaching or rebuking or judging; Nephi sees Him "ministering unto the people" (1 Ne. 11:27). When Christ appears to the Nephites, He ministers to the afflicted, and "both they who had been healed and they who were whole, [did] bow down and worship him" (3 Ne. 17:10). We are born into a world suffused by suffering. We carry in our bodies, in our genetic makeup, the pain and trauma incident to mortality. As agents, and as beings subject to the agency of others, we act and are acted upon in a world of hurt and handicap. As we saw in the religious history recounted previously, the trauma and wounds in our lives have often multiplied, been augmented rather than alleviated by the religious traditions we inherit. For the majority of the world's inhabitants, and for most of us striving to find joy in the gospel, a great portion of our lives is a protracted exercise in pain management.

The trauma so prevalent in society is not just the domain of veterans with PTSD or refugees from a war zone. It's here, "even at our doors," in middle-class America. As the author and psychiatrist Dr. Bessel van der Kolk states, "One does not have to be a combat soldier, or visit a refugee camp in Syria or the Congo to encounter trauma. Trauma happens to us, our friends, our families, and our neighbors." He argues that much of the behavior we see as deviant, unhealthy, or in any way disruptive or criminal can be traced back to trauma experienced by people at some point in their lives. Brokenness, not sinfulness, is our general condition; healing from trauma is what is needed.[4] Deanna Thompson says it most simply: "All of our lives bear the marks of suffering."[5] Toni Morrison's writings are poignant meditations on this truth: "Cycles of violence play out across generations. The wounds do not simply go away."[6] The biblical scholar David Bentley Hart argues that this view of sin is in fact truer to Paul's original language in Romans: "Paul speaks of . . . sin as a kind of contagion, a disease with which all are born; . . . but never as an inherited condition of criminal culpability."[7]

Simply put: as Julian sensed, woundedness is the collateral damage that is essential to our learning process along the path to life eternal. Woundedness is essential and inevitable in the Great Plan's unfolding. It is through our necessary experience of the bitter that we may learn to prize the sweetness of what is good and pure and beautiful—the sweetness that is Christ. Sin, which in the book of Moses is associated with "the bitter," is what we taste so that we may learn to recognize and avoid it and cleave to the sweetness of Christ and his precepts. The whole point of our participation in sin is to learn, to experience, and to be personally, empirically educated in the beauty of Christ's way. By our immersion in a world of choice and consequences, we learn that certain choices we make and, as often, consequences we suffer at the hands of others, take us to a place that is "contrary to the nature of happiness" (Alma 41:11).

Five centuries after Julian of Norwich, a French philosopher returned to Julian's question, intuiting more fully what she sensed:

> Wouldn't it have been simpler for God to have created a perfect world? . . . The new-born baby is profoundly incomplete, but it is exactly because of this that he can go so much farther than a young animal, for liberty is tied to "unperfectedness." From his unperfected state, man gives rise to infinite possibilities. He makes of his weakness a strength; of his unperfected state, free agency. Is it not this that helps us to understand why God made this unperfected world?[8]

Mortality is that school in which we learn to exercise our agency wisely and magnanimously. It is inescapable that in this learning process we will both incur and inflict pain. As Francine Bennion reminded us, "we were willing to *know* hunger. Like Christ in the desert, we did not ask God to let us try falling or being bruised only on condition that he catch us before we touch ground and save us from real hurt. We were willing to *know* hurt."[9]

At the same time, even as we are given the liberty to act for ourselves, to choose—that liberty is generally untutored, compromised, or otherwise mitigated. As Hart notes, unimpaired moral agency "is a manifest falsehood. There is no such thing as perfect freedom in this life, or perfect understanding, and it is sheer nonsense to suggest that we possess limitless or unqualified liberty. Therefore we are incapable of contracting a limitless or unqualified guilt. *There are always extenuating circumstances*" (his emphasis).[10] Heavenly Parents anticipate the wounds incident to that learning process. Understanding the inescapability of that educative design invites us to reconsider the label so drenched in connotations of the vile, the evil, the malicious.

A little history of usage may be helpful in reinforcing this view. The word translated as "sin" in the New Testament is *hamartia* (ἁμαρτία). It appears in a critical place in ancient usage, and anyone who can remember their high school English class can probably call to mind the word's common meaning: the so-called tragic flaw of a heroic character was called *hamartia*. Here is the powerful insight: when the popularizer of this idea, the Greek philosopher Aristotle, used the term, he used it *not* in reference to a flaw in *character* but to a flaw in one's *choice*. (Tragic harm occurs "not due to any moral defect or depravity, but to an error.")[11] *Hamartia* means a "misstep," or a "missing of the mark." In the book of Moses, sin is presented as a misdirection, as employing choice in ways contrary to the nature of happiness. N. T. Wright gives an apt analogy: "When God looks at sin, what he sees is what a violin maker would see if the player were to use his lovely creation as a tennis racquet."[12] Such missteps are a necessary part of our education. They are to be expected. They do not make us criminals deserving retribution. They reveal us as souls in need of redirection.

A most important consequence of this reorientation in understanding sin is the effect it can have on the compassion with
which we view ourselves and each other. When the angel referred
to the world of today as being in a "state of awful woundedness,"
he provided a term, *woundedness*, that is accurate and is a catalyst
to love. First, its accuracy: Embodiment in corruptible flesh and
blood does not entail the inheritance of Adamic sin, though it does
entail the inheritance of physical, psychological, and emotional
traits passed down through genetic family structures together with
the vicissitudes of environment. While agency is, for Latter-day
Saints, the most prized God-given gift, it is mitigated by the
factors mentioned previously. In Paul's concise metaphor, we see
ourselves—and others—"by means of a mirror obscurely" (1 Cor.
13:12, Wuest trans.). Imperfectly.

Second, seeing our condition as wounded is a spur to charity
rather than to judgment. The impact of seeing the "sinner" as the
"wounded" is profound and meaningful in the here and now.
This perspective is not an abstract theological prescription but a
recipe for a more vibrant and caring discipleship in the present
world. In the Christian past, sin was equated with a contagion.
Even now, hearing that a person is mired in sin, we tend to label,
to retreat, to avoid, to shun. If we hear instead that the individual
is deeply wounded, our heart is drawn out in compassion, and
our inclination is to succor and heal. Categories like "the saved"
and "the damned," "the sinner" and "the righteous," erect boundaries and invite judgment. Recognizing the universality of our
woundedness and the universal love of God invites community
and mutual concern.

In the classic film *It's a Wonderful Life*, the angel Clarence
must find a way to rescue George Bailey from his suicidal despair.
Unexpectedly, he finds the solution in his own leap into the dark
abyss of water Bailey is contemplating. Bailey immediately moves
to rescue the fallen angel. A fellow traveler's vulnerability has

shattered the shell of his own self-concern. As children of Divine
Parents, we, too, are powerfully drawn to succor the marginalized,
the wounded, the broken, the vulnerable.

Shelly Rambo records how, through her studies of trauma, "I
view persons as more vulnerable . . . and the earth more wounded
than I did before." She adds, "I have come to believe that we are
more connected in ways that we cannot account for and constituted
by much that we do not know."[13] Truly, as Serena Jones writes:

> It is hard to think of a task more central to Christian the-
> ology than this one: finding the language to speak grace in
> a form that allows it to come toward humanity in ways as
> gentle as they are powerful. . . . If the church's message about
> God's love for the world is to be offered to those who suffer
> these wounds, then we must think anew about how we use
> language and how we put bodies in motion and employ
> imagery and sound. With fresh openness we must grapple
> with the meaning of beliefs not only about grace, but also
> about such matters as sin."[14]

Flora Keshgegian agrees: "If Christianity is to be a religion
of remembering for witness and transformation, then it needs
to change from its focus on sin and death to an affirmation of
creation and life."[15]

None of this is to say that we are not capable of sin in the
sense of a deliberately chosen action that is wrong and harmful.
We clearly are. We are complex beings, with complex motivations, and we are seldom wholly guilty or wholly innocent of
any misdeed. As Immanuel Kant argued with irrefutable logic,
guilt is the recognition that we *should* have, and therefore *could*
have, acted differently.[16] In other words, we are never utterly de-
prived of the power "to choose liberty and eternal life"; however
impaired, disadvantaged by others, weakened or diminished by

circumstance or inheritance, we are always, to some degree, "free . . . to act for [our]selves" (2 Ne. 2:27; Hel. 14:30). This knowledge that our heavenly parents intend for us to "act not [merely] to be acted upon" is both comforting and empowering (2 Ne. 2:13). Since we are apprentices of eternal life, remorse for falling short along the path is an appropriate response. Not guilt, if by *guilt* we mean the preoccupation with unworthiness that is self-concerned and unproductive. Remorse, by contrast, is other-concerned and is evidence of an empathy productive of greater holiness.

NOTES

1   B. R. Rees, *Pelagius: Life and Letters* (Woodbridge, UK: Boydell, 1991), 127.

2   Krister Stendahl, *Paul among Jews and Gentiles* (Philadelphia: Fortress, 1976), 40–41, 85.

3   Denise N. Baker, ed., *The Showings of Julian of Norwich*, 13.27 (New York: Norton, 2005), 39.

4   Bessel van der Kolk, *The Body Keeps the Score: Brain, Mind and Body in the Healing of Trauma* (New York: Viking, 2015), 1.

5   Deanna A. Thompson, "Faith in a Traumatized World," Brigham Young University Humanities Colloquium, February 13, 2020.

6   Shelly Rambo, "How Christian Theology and Practice Are Being Shaped by Trauma Studies: Talking about God in the Face of Wounds That Won't Go Away," *The Christian Century*, November 1, 2019, https://www.christiancentury.org/article/critical-essay/how-christian-theology-and-practice-are-being-shaped-trauma-studies.

7   David Bentley Hart, *The New Testament: A Translation* (New Haven: Yale University Press, 2017), 296–297.

8   Jean-Claude Barreau, *Où est le mal?*, trans. Jeremy Dick (Paris: Seuil, 1969), 49–50.

9   Francine R. Bennion, "A Latter-day Saint Theology of Suffering," in *At the Pulpit*, ed. Jennifer Reeder and Kate Holbrook (Salt Lake City: Church Historian's Press, 2017), 224.

10   David Bentley Hart, *That All Shall Be Saved: Heaven, Hell, and Universal Salvation* (New Haven: Yale University Press, 2019), 38.

11   Aristotle, *Poetics* 7.2 (New York: Penguin, 1996), 21. In this immensely influential work, which set the parameters of subsequent literary theory, Aristotle deals with ἁμαρτία in his section on a play's action ("tragic plot"). The term is not employed in the section on "character." The "sin" is in the ill-considered action, not a personal defect, in spite of what thousands of English teachers have taught through the decades.

12   N. T. Wright, *The Day the Revolution Began* (New York: HarperCollins, 2010), 132.

13   Shelly Rambo, *Spirit and Trauma: A Theology of Remaining* (Louisville, KY: Westminster John Knox, 2010), xiii–xiv.

14   Serene Jones, *Trauma and Grace: Theology in a Ruptured World* (Louisville, KY: Westminster John Knox, 2009), xxii, 11.

15   Flora A. Keshgegian, *Redeeming Memories: A Theology of Healing and Transformation* (Nashville: Abingdon Press, 2000), 158.

16   Those who are "censured as guilty of their crimes" and "find these censures as well founded" are implicitly recognizing that those actions arose "from one's choice" with a "basis in free causality." Immanuel Kant, *Critique of Practical Reason* 5:100 (Cambridge: Cambridge University Press, 2015), 81.

CHAPTER TEN

Justice

From Punishment to Restoration

And what of justice? Sin may be an errant step, but it is still violation of a law. And does that violation not warrant punishment? "Every transgression of the law deserves punishment," declares a representative Protestant handbook.[1] As far back as the early fifth century, Pelagius was lamenting the direction in which such thinking was taking the church: "Oh horror!, we ascribe iniquity to the righteous and cruelty to the holy, . . . so that God . . . seems to have sought not so much our salvation as our punishment!"[2]

As mortals, we have a strong sense of justice, which is often just a thin veneer covering our own desire for vicarious retribution. Sometimes, there isn't even a veneer; as the English theologian William Paley wrote, "by the satisfaction of justice, I mean the retribution of so much pain for so much guilt; which . . . we expect at the hand of God, and which we are accustomed to consider as the order of things that perfect justice dictates and requires."[3] Of course, as Friedrich Nietzsche pointed out, the perverse logic of this mathematical conception assumes that the pleasure of retribution is needful to cancel out the pain of the offense.[4] Worlds hang in the balance when definitions of justice are at stake. One scholar notes how a definition of justice as retributive punishment is deeply ingrained in our cultural practices: "The criminal justice system of the United States operates on the principle of retribution. This system operates under the assumption that doing justice means to inflict punishment, which is understood as violence. The assumption is that small crimes require small penalties, while a big crime requires a big penalty. The biggest punishment, namely death, is reserved for the most heinous crimes. . . . The assumption of retributive justice—that doing justice means [meting] out punishment—is virtually universal among North Americans."[5] And the roots of retributive justice, as we have seen, are thoroughly religious, embedded most particularly in the Protestant theology of atonement (see chapter 13).

There is something mean-spirited about the way we generally employ the term *justice*, not only because it often conceals a human thirst for retribution but also because we use it as a form of self-validation. Christian theologians and preachers openly professed that part of heaven's joy would include our ability to see the suffering of the damned in hell ("in order that the happiness of the saints may be more delightful to them and that they may render more copious thanks to God for it, they are allowed to see perfectly the sufferings of the damned," wrote Thomas Aquinas).[6] Alerting us to related motivations, Jesus warned against the elder-brother-of-the-prodigal-son syndrome. In the parable of the laborers in the vineyard (Matt. 20:1–16) we see the petty indignation of the longtime workers who are resentful that the latecomers receive the same pay. In the story of Jonah, we see the prophet on the front row to witness Nineveh's destruction (Jonah 4). Both of these stories are about the demand for recognition, status, or preeminence, masquerading as the call for "justice." Owen Barfield sees what is happening here: Jesus is deliberately "outraging" our "deep-rooted feeling for the goodness of justice and equity . . . because we are being beckoned towards a position directionally opposite to the usual one; because we are invited to see the earth, for a moment at all events, rather as it must look from the sun;

to experience the world of man as the object of a huge, positive outpouring of love, in the flood of whose radiance such trifles as merit and recompense are mere irrelevancies."[7]

Dostoevsky pointed out the fruitlessness of justice as retribution. As his character Ivan cries out to his brother, "What use is vengeance to me, what use to me is hell for torturers, what can hell put right again? . . . I don't want anyone to suffer anymore."[8] This is the topic that occupies Alma in his great discourse on the subject, delivered to his troubled son Corianton. Why, his son wonders, must punishment follow misconduct? Especially because, as we discussed previously, God is not affronted by anything we can do. Their honor is not threatened, and They do not demand our punishment. As Paul taught, *nothing* "shall be able to separate us from the love of God, which is in Christ Jesus our Lord" (Rom. 8:39). Julian of Norwich wisely wrote that "it is [Satan's] meaning to make us so heavy and so sorrowful in this that we [are not able to see] the blessed beholding of our everlasting Friend. . . . Our falling does not prevent him from loving us."[9]

The false traditions of the fathers are unflagging in their assertions that punishment is God's "justice." The Book of Mormon, however, gives us a radically different way to think about justice. And the central concept in that scriptural framework is *agency*. No other religious tradition has made agency so central to its theological understanding. "God gave unto man that he should act for himself," said Lehi (2 Ne. 2:16). But that freedom to choose is always the freedom to choose *something*. Alma calls this principle, the principle by which every choice brings about a consequence that is tied to it, "the plan of restoration" because we shall have "restored" to us that which we most desire (Alma 41:2). As we manifest our "desires of happiness, or . . . desires of good," then we are "raised to happiness . . . or good" accordingly (verse 5). Julian of Norwich wisely perceived that in most of us is a "godly will that never assents to sin nor ever shall."[10] Pico della

Mirandola, who loved this same principle, exclaimed, "O great and wonderful happiness of man. It is given to him to have that which he desires and to be that which he wills."[11] It is precisely *this principle* that the Book of Mormon calls "the justice of God." In *this* essential regard, justice works *in* our favor. (For when it does *not,* see chapter 11, "Repentance.") Justice is the principle by which God assures us that They will stand as surety behind this law of restoration. And this explains why Latter-day Saint scripture twice refers to such agency as a supernal gift (D&C 101:78; Moses 7:32). As B. H. Roberts wrote, this "inexorableness of law is at once both its majesty and glory." Because within its domain we can choose with full "sense of security, . . . safety . . . and rational faith."[12] Because of the law of restoration we can be assured that we will have "good for that which is good; righteous for that which is righteous; just for that which is just; merciful for that which is merciful" (Alma 41:13).

While it is true that to choose to indulge a desire is to choose its fruit—bitter or sweet—accountability depends upon, as Lehi taught, *their being "instructed sufficiently"* to understand what they are choosing (2 Ne. 2:5). But the crucial caveat is this: never in this life do we attain perfect understanding and a will utterly uncontaminated by all kinds of white noise. And yet, noted the early Christian Maximus the Confessor, "the 'natural will' within us, which is the rational ground of our whole power of volition, must tend only toward God as its true end. . . . The rational soul cannot really will the evil as truly evil." In short, "sin requires some degree of ignorance, and ignorance is by definition a diverting of the mind and will to an end they would not naturally pursue."[13]

This is why, when we use our agency wrongly, it creates an occasion for God's mercy to enter in: not because our guilt is excused but because our guilt is seldom entire in the first place. This is a recognition of seismic significance. As our desires evolve in more righteous directions, our choices become wiser and more informed by truth and light and love. We become more accountable as our agency grows more refined. Our Heavenly Parents thus assume a very different role in the drama of human choice and consequence. They counsel, educate, inform, instruct, guide, and encourage us to make those choices that will eventuate in the sweet rather than the bitter. John assigns this task of guiding and encouraging principally to the Holy Spirit, who will "teach [us] all things" and serve as our "Comforter" along the journey (John 14:26).

NOTES

1   Alan Richardson and John Bowden, eds., *The Westminster Dictionary of Christian Theology* (Philadelphia: Westminster Press, 1983), 539.

2   Pelagius, "Letter to Demetrias," in Stuart Squires, *The Pelagian Controversy: An Introduction to the Enemies of Grace and the Conspiracy of Lost Souls* (Eugene, OR: Pickwick, 2019), 111.

3   William Paley, *Works* (London: Longman, 1838), 3:298–99.

4   Nietzsche makes this argument at length in the second chapter of his work *The Genealogy of Morals* (1887). His point of departure is the dual meaning of the German *Schuld* as both "debt" and "guilt."

5   J. Denny Weaver, "Violence in Christian Theology," *Cross Currents* (Summer 2001): 155–56.

6   Thomas Aquinas, *Summa Theologica*, Suppl. Tertia Partis, Q. 94 Art. 1 (New York: Benziger Brothers, 1948), 3:2972.

7   Owen Barfield, *Saving the Appearances: A Study in Idolatry* (Middletown, CT: Wesleyan University Press, 1988), 174.

8   Fyodor Dostoyevsky, *The Brothers Karamazov* (New York: Penguin, 2003), 320.

9   Denise N. Baker, ed., *The Showings of Julian of Norwich*, 16.76 and 13.39 (New York: Norton, 2005), 115, 49. We have modernized the spelling and at times modified the translation.

10   Baker, *Showings of Julian of Norwich*, 13.37, p. 51.

11   Pico della Mirandola, "Oration on the Dignity of Man," cited in Diarmaid MacCulloch, *The Reformation: A History* (New York: Viking, 2004), 103.

12   B. H. Roberts, *The Way, the Truth, and the Life: An Elementary Treatise on Theology*, ed. John Welch (Provo, UT: BYU Studies, 1994), 404.

13   David Bentley Hart, *That All Shall Be Saved: Heaven, Hell, and Universal Salvation* (New Haven: Yale University Press, 2019), 36.

CHAPTER ELEVEN

Repentance

From Looking Back to Looking Forward

A s we noted in the previous chapter, justice works in our favor. It is our guarantee that we will be "raised to happiness according to our desires of happiness" (Alma 41:5). The problem, of course, is that our desires are sometimes muddled, confused, misdirected. Our entire relationship with God will change when we are able to recognize that repentance is not the discipline meted out to us when we get it wrong; repentance is the lifelong venture of accepting Christ's willingness to help us shape our heart in his image. It is a positive engagement with the learning process, not recurrent periods in the penalty box. In the scriptures, one episode more than any other may illustrate how Jesus taught the principle. In the Gospel of John the story unfolds of a woman caught in adultery. The crowd gathers, intent on executing "justice." Christ, with one simple gesture, repudiates their retributive justice and teaches the meaning of repentance: "Neither do I condemn thee." Jesus continues, "Go, and sin no more" (John 8:11). *That* is repentance: continuation of the journey, picking ourselves up and moving forward, energized and renewed by the certainty of God's abiding love and encouragement. As a student remarked of this episode, "Christ shows no interest in official church discipline or forgiving the woman for her past. Rather, he desires change and conversion for the woman."[1]

The entire Great Plan is predicated on our Heavenly Parents' confidence that through the process of our mortal experiences we will learn to choose more wisely and that our desires, our yearnings, our affections, will become more and more centered on the Good, the True, the Beautiful. In other words, under the tutelage of divinity, we are encouraged to persevere in the often painful path home. The constant ministrations ("I will never leave thee, nor forsake thee" [Heb. 13:5]) of the Divine Family strengthen our knees and lift our hands when they hang down. Hence the constant refrain that weaves through scripture as its most common theme: "repent"; that is, "reeducate" or "reset your heart."

We discussed previously that sin is not first and foremost an offense against a sovereign God; it is a tragic misstep, an action contrary to the nature of happiness, resulting in pain, suffering, alienation—that is, bitterness. We also discussed previously that justice is not God's demand for satisfaction of a law violated; it is a law of restoration, of like for like, of consequence fitted to desire. Repentance may require restitution where possible; repairing what harm we can is a sign of our genuine remorse and empathy. Repentance, however, is not penance (self-punishment), though it regrettably still carries those connotations. The indelible association of repentance with penance is rooted in a historic mistranslation. In the fourth century, Jerome produced a Latin translation of the Bible that would serve as the standard Christian text for more than a thousand years. A scholar of the Reformation explains what happened when Jerome came to the moment in Matthew 3:2 "where John the Baptist is presented in the Greek as crying out to his listeners in the wilderness: 'metanoeite.' Jerome translated this as *poenitentiam agite*, 'do penance,' and the medieval Church had pointed to this translation of the Baptist's cry as biblical support for its theology of the sacrament of penance."[2]

Penance has the same root as *penal* and *penalty*—the Latin *poenalis*, which means "pertaining to punishment." Underlying this sacrament of penance, then, is the rationale that sin is primarily an offense committed against God and that a penalty must be paid to "obtain pardon" for that offense.[3] In the words of another expositor of the doctrine, absolution "tak[es] away the individual's sin and mak[es] him guiltless before God. [Then comes] satisfaction—the acts the sinner has to perform to compensate for the injury he has done to God."[4] How dreadful that an invitation to change one's heart became instead a demand for punishment. In the sixteenth century, the progressive Catholic theologian Erasmus pointed out that what "John had told his listeners to do was *to come to their senses*, or repent, and Erasmus re-translated the command into Latin as *resipiscite* [repent, in English]." In other words, with this one biblical revision, Erasmus shifted the emphasis from punishment for the past to transformation going forward. What a difference one word makes for good or ill.[5]

Still, the older implications linger. Calvin taught that "repentance stemmed from serious fear of God and consisted in the mortification of the old man."[6] And indeed, many Saints live in fear of violation, trespass, offense, or crime, and the ensuing guilt. Collectively or individually, many are at every moment fearful of an offended God, an "injured" sovereign, who demands "satisfaction." Erasmus incurred the wrath of the institutional church for his simple correction. However, he was right. Repentance, rather than entailing a sacrament of penance and absolution, is a call to "come to your senses," as he correctly interpreted the Greek term.[7] Note here the echo of Lehi's admonition to "awake, awake from a deep sleep" (2 Ne. 1:13) and Jacob's call to "arouse the faculties of your souls; shake yourselves that ye may awake" (Jacob 3:11). The call of John the Baptist in the book of Matthew is identical to the call of Paul to the Romans: "Do not be conformed to this world, but be transformed by the renewing of your minds, so that you may discern what is the will of God—what is good and acceptable and perfect" (Rom. 12:2). Or, as the original might be more fully rendered, "Do not allow yourself to be shaped and fashioned by the world in which you find yourself, but be *rebirthed in mind and will* [*anakainosei tou noos*], that you may *sample first-hand through trial and error* [*dokimadzein*] what is God's desire for you: the Good, the well-pleasing, the full measure of your creation [*teleion*]."[8] This language should suggest to Latter-day Saints a ringing affirmation of the original proposal conceived in heaven: that we be exposed to a world of oppositional choices, that we taste the bitter and the sweet, and that we allow those experiences to shape our heart and mind after a holy pattern, so that we can attain our full stature as children of Heavenly Parents.

This is our challenge, our task: to learn, through painful experience, the true nature and consequences of our choices, the reality of sweetness and bitterness as indissolubly connected to eternal principles. It is a long process, and we are going through it until we are able—here or hereafter—to choose Christ with eyes fully opened, the bitter rejected and the sweet embraced. We are "whole from the foundation" of the world. But as we come to live in a sphere where chaos reigns, ensouled in bodies subject to all that is "carnal" and "sensual," tempted by all that appeals to our biologically inherited natures, we taste the bitter fruit in order to learn to prize the sweet. This process of reeducating our inclinations is one way to translate very literally *repentance*. Reeducation of the heart. Remolding of desires. We hear echoes of these phrases in God's encouragement to "set your affections on things above" (Col. 3:2), or to "let the affections of thy heart be placed upon the Lord" (Alma 37:36).

At some level, most Latter-day Saints understand this process. We strive for a devotion born of love, and we worship Heavenly Parents who seek our joy. Why then are we so saddled with self-doubt, with guilt, with feelings of unworthiness, shame, and fear of judgment? Somewhere, in the back of our minds, the image of a God of Justice, who requires penance and grudgingly dispenses forgiveness, stubbornly persists. We continue to feel, and act, as if God requires repentance to put us right with Them; to assuage Their offended Majesty; to compensate for the injury done to Them; to "pay" for our sins. And centuries of representations of this idea of repentance reinforce the sense of threat God poses to our peace of mind. Even in our own Latter-day Saint culture, we can draw the wrong inferences from our dogged attempts to conceptualize the Atonement as Christ rescuing us from God's justice, or as Christ interceding as our defender, protecting us from the angry Judge eager to impose penalty. We saw how the Book of Mormon suppresses the savagery of a retributive "justice," and we forget or may not know that *advocate* has a genealogy traceable to the Greek word that means "comforter" or "helper." We are still, regrettably, far from successful in displacing the Sovereign God of creedal Christianity with the restored plain and precious truth that God is the Father and Mother who "are reaching across . . . streams and mountains and deserts, anxious to hold [us] close."[9]

From God's perspective, sin is of concern because of the havoc it wreaks in us and because of the harm it causes us to do to ourselves and to each other. In God's vocabulary, sin is suffering, woundedness, and brokenness in our relationships. Knowing this, how can we ever see sin, or the need for repentance, as we did before?

NOTES

    1   Josh Davis, "Confess Them and Forsake Them" (unpublished manuscript, December 2019).

    2   Diarmaid MacCulloch, *The Reformation: A History* (New York: Viking, 2004), 96.

3   J. Dallen, "Penance, Sacrament of," in *New Catholic Encyclopedia* (Detroit: Gale, 2003), 11:66.

4   Michael Massing, *Fatal Discord: Erasmus, Luther, and the Fight for the Western Mind* (New York: HarperCollins, 2018), 52.

5   MacCulloch, *Reformation*, 96.

6   Walter A. Elwell, ed., "Repentance," in *Evangelical Dictionary of Theology* (Grand Rapids, MI: Baker Academic, 2001), 1012.

7   Massing, *Fatal Discord*, 325.

8   Terryl's translation.

9   Jeffrey R. Holland, "Belonging: A View of Membership," *Ensign*, April 1980, 27.

CHAPTER TWELVE

Forgiveness

From Transactional Love to Absolute Love

What, then, does it mean to forgive? In the conventional telling of the Eden story, the original sin is an outrage against a sovereign master. In Dante's calculus of sin and punishment, humankind's offense against a perfect God was infinitely vile and so required an infinite payment in punishment—which humans cannot provide. "For no obedience, no humility, / he offered later could have been so deep / that it could match the heights he meant to reach / through disobedience."[1] And so, according to the traditional telling, Christ steps between us and God's wrath, absorbing the penalty on the cross. All of this, of course, comes as the ripple effects of what is seen as Eve's disobedience.

In the Restoration revision to the story, Eve's action was a noble gesture that launched the great cosmic enterprise. Eve introduced us to a world of experiences, both sweet and bitter. So in the restored Church what meaning does forgiveness have? And why must God forgive us if most of our offenses are against other mortals? "Where is the harmony" to be found, in either punishment or forgiveness, asked Dostoevsky's Ivan.

The Greek word most commonly used for *forgive* is the same as the word sometimes translated as *remit*: *aphiemi* (ἀφίημι). Its primary meaning is "to let go" or "to lay aside." This meaning works perfectly well to capture the essence of most human forgiveness.

We lay aside that hurt, that resentment, or even that memory, which dams up the flow of brotherly love. Sin and forgiveness alike might be profitably reframed by considering the aptly named "olive leaf" revelation, the "Lord's message of peace" to his people. Here we learn about the "glory of the celestial kingdom" of which the Comforter is "the promise" and foretaste. We are then given to understand that the Light and Love of Jesus Christ bathe the entire universe:

> He is in the sun, and the light of the sun, and the power thereof by which it was made. As also he is in the moon, and is the light of the moon, and the power thereof by which it was made; As also the light of the stars, and the power thereof by which they were made; And the earth also, and the power thereof, even the earth upon which you stand. And the light which shineth, which giveth you light, is through him who enlighteneth your eyes, which is the same light that quickeneth your understandings; Which light proceedeth forth from the presence of God to fill the immensity of space—The light which is in all things, . . . giveth life to all things. (D&C 88:7–13)

This holy influence, this "light of Christ," is actually made synonymous with His very person: "He that ascended up on high, as also he descended below all things, in that he comprehended all things, that he might be in all and through all things, the light of truth; Which . . . *is* the light of Christ." As we saw in Nephi's vision, God the Heavenly Son, incarnate as the babe of Bethlehem, was the embodiment of perfect love—a love of infinite power to permeate the universe of all things and persons, uniting all in a heavenly Zion, a holy community, the church of the Firstborn.

Why, then, is our human community fractured, broken, disunited? The instinctive answer is sin. However, that answer substitutes a cliché for an explanation. Communities, nations, families, friendships, and relationships of every kind are wounded—shattered, even—when the bonds of human affection are damaged by resentment, suspicion, jealousy, anger, and a thousand other impediments to love. Sin is the name we give to the myriad choices we make that disrupt the irradiation of the universe by Christ's perfectly unifying, bonding selfless love. In other words, *when we sin we erect barriers to the flow of Christ's life-affirming and life-uniting light.* Our trespasses, *from this perspective,* are the rocks that block the current of love that proceeds "from the presence of God to fill the immensity of space." Harmful actions are the blockage, the impediments we create to God's designs for a universal harmony.

We are the channels through whom God's love passes to another, and hence God's greatest concern is that we do not obstruct the flow; forgiveness clears the channels for Their love to emanate freely. One of the most astonishing things Joseph said about the celestial kingdom is this: "If you do not accuse each other God will not accuse you. If you have no accuser you will enter heaven."[2] This statement reflects a peculiarly Latter-day Saint version of heaven: someone's refusal to forgive me impedes our relationship and in that way constrains my heaven as well as hers. This is hard doctrine. Regardless of my personal sanctity or righteousness, I cannot experience a celestial existence if love does not flow without inhibition between myself and all members of that heavenly community. Because, as we discussed earlier, authentic, loving relationships are not preparation for heaven—they constitute heaven. In a very real sense, our own willingness to set aside our hurts and injuries has a direct, essential bearing on the quality of that heaven enjoyed by others—and vice versa.

Can God set aside our sins, as we set aside those of our offenders? The answer to this question is suggested by Jesus when He taught us to pray that we might be forgiven "*as we forgive* our debtors" (Matt. 6:12). In other words, God is able to set aside our offenses in the same way in which we set aside those of others. "The nearer we get to our Heavenly Father," testified Joseph, "the more we are disposed to look with compassion on perishing souls; we feel that we want to take them on our shoulders, and *cast their sins behind our backs*."[3] That is the essence of forgiveness. This principle is reaffirmed explicitly by Paul, who wrote the Corinthians explaining that one way Christ atones, or "reconciles" the world unto himself, is simply by "not imputing their trespasses unto them" (2 Cor. 5:19). In another, more vivid rendering of that verse, "Christ was reconciling the world to himself, not putting down on the liability side of their ledger their trespasses" (2 Cor. 5:18–19; Wuest). Forgiveness, writes Henri Nouwen, "demands of me that I step over that wounded part of my heart that feels hurt and wronged and that wants to . . . put a few conditions between me and the one whom I am asked to forgive. This 'stepping over' is the authentic [practice] of forgiveness."[4]

Is this really the same pattern for God's forgiveness of us? Doesn't scripture say that "ye may know if a man repenteth of his sins [if] he will confess them and forsake them"? (D&C 58:43). While that scripture is valid, the meaning may be otherwise than we have supposed: Confessing and forsaking are not the stages of repentance; they are evidence of a change of heart that has already occurred. They are not the preconditions for God's forgiveness. As Wuest translates Christ's final words to the Apostles as they departed on their own healing ministries, any sins "you forgive, . . . have been previously forgiven them, . . . they are in a state of forgiveness" (John 20:22). Christ has already opened the gates of heaven to us. The Wisdom of Solomon was a book of tremendous influence in the early Christian Church and is found in the Apocrypha (which contains "many things" that "are true," according to D&C 91:1). The author of Wisdom celebrated a God in this mold: "You are merciful to all, for you can do all things, and you overlook people's sins, *so that they may repent*, for you love all things that exist" (Wisdom 11:23–24; our emphasis).

Christ has already laid our trespasses aside. As Wendell Berry wrote of his own mother (which mother's love, says Elder Holland, is the nearest to Christ's redemptive love[5]):

> So complete has your forgiveness been
>
> I wonder sometimes if it did not
>
> precede my wrong, and I erred,
>
> safe found, within your love.[6]

If we fail to see the father of the prodigal son as our own Heavenly Parent, we have missed the story's import. Henri Nouwen writes, our Heavenly Father "has no desire to punish [His children]. They have already been punished excessively by their own inner or outer waywardness. The Father wants simply to let them know that the love they have searched for . . . has been, is, and always will be there for them."[7]

NOTES

1   Dante, *Paradiso* 7.97–101, trans. Allen Mandelbaum (New York: Bantam, 1984).

2   "History, 1838–1856, volume C-1 Addenda," p. 20, The Joseph Smith Papers, accessed October 25, 2019, https://www.josephsmithpapers .org/paper-summary/history-1838-1856-volume-c-1-addenda/20.

3   From a sermon given to the Relief Society, 9 June 1842, in Jill Mulvay Derr, et al., *The First Fifty Years of Relief Society: Key Documents in Latter-day Saint Women's History* (Salt Lake City: Church Historians Press, 2016), 78

4   Henri J. M. Nouwen, *The Return of the Prodigal Son: A Story of Homecoming* (New York: Doubleday, 1994), 130.

5   Jeffrey Holland, "Behold Thy Mother," *Ensign* 45, no. 11 (November 2015).

6   Wendell Berry, "To My Mother," in *New Collected Poems* (Berkeley: Counterpoint, 2012), 319.

7   Nouwen, *Return of the Prodigal*, 96.

CHAPTER THIRTEEN

Atonement

From Penal Substitution to Radical Healing

Few Christian doctrines have come under such concerted attack in recent years as the doctrine of atonement, which Stephen Finlan refers to as an "embarrassment among Christians." In his work on the subject, he notes the growing view that "a compassionate God is . . . incompatible with all atonement theories."[1] To the extent that those theories bear the traces of medieval and Reformation assumptions alike, we agree. We do not agree with Finlan's conclusion but understand why he would feel driven to jettison the whole project: "Atonement is not an essential doctrine of Christianity."[2] How can we return to a healthier and truer conception?

Many ideas that Latter-day Saints hold about atonement are in fact products of that same Reformation era that left such widespread theological carnage. A review of the historical evolution of that *most* essential doctrine, the doctrine of the Atonement, requires a long digression but is necessary to understand the roots of our own ideas and language on the subject. And the following review may help us sort out how we can return to a conception generative of greater peace and hope.

In the earliest Christian writings on the subject, Eve and Adam (and by inheritance, all their posterity) fell into Satan's power by sinning. They thereby became his captives in hell. In this "ransom theory," God tricked Satan by offering Jesus as payment for humanity's debt. In Gregory of Nyssa's conception, Christ was "the bait" that enticed Satan to accept the deal; unaware of Christ's divinity, the devil "swallowed [the hook], he was caught straightaway [and] the bars of hell were burst."[3] In the middle ages, Anselm revised the model from ransom theory to satisfaction theory in accordance with medieval notions of honor and feudal obligation. As he wrote, "To sin is to fail to render to God His due. What is due to God? Righteousness, or rectitude of will. He who fails to render this honor to God, robs God of that which belongs to Him and dishonors God. . . . And what is satisfaction? . . . More than what was taken away must be rendered back." Only Christ, as human, could share in the debt, and only Christ, as God, could restore God's honor. Thus, only Christ as man-God could accomplish atonement. Christ died in our place to satisfy the debt of an offended honor.[4]

With the Reformation, legalism replaces feudalism, and we see the development of penal substitution as the primary variant of satisfaction theory. God is the embodiment of justice, and as such, He demands a payment for violation of the law. Jesus is sacrificed in our place—this is the doctrine of penal substitution. In Calvin's words, Jesus "by his sacrifice, appeased the divine anger; by his blood, washed away our stains; by his cross, bore our curse; and by his death, made satisfaction for us."[5] Or in Luther's language, "For we are sinners and thieves, and therefore guilty of death and everlasting damnation." In our place, "God hath laid our sins, not upon us, but upon his Son, Christ."[6] In Tyndale's language, we need Christ to save us "from the vengeance of the law." "His blood, his death, . . . appeased the wrath of God."[7]

Notice several implications of this model, which the Saints regrettably generally accept unquestioningly: Sin is offense against God and demands punishment; it is not a misstep or educative experience of the bitter. Justice is retribution for that offense; it is "vengeance," rather than a principle of restoration that operates in accord with our evolving desires and yearnings. God is angry and wrathful toward us and our sins, but He is mollified by seeing Jesus suffer in our place. Jesus is our shield against God's vengeance. In sum, the phrase "*penal* substitution" reveals the utter dependence of this atonement theory on a model of criminality and punishment. As René Gerard remarked, "God feels the need to revenge his honour, which has been tainted by the sins of humanity. . . . Not only does God require a . . . victim, but he requires the victim who is most precious and dear to him, his very own son." Gerard concludes with tragic truth: "No doubt this line of reasoning has done more than anything else to discredit Christianity in the eyes of the people of good will in the modern world."[8]

These ideas are indeed jarring to modern sensibilities; in fact, they are increasingly becoming an "embarrassment among Christians" and have prompted a range of new atonement theologies. J. Denny Weaver advocates an approach to atonement and Christology that "does not presume justice depends on punishment, that does not put God in the role of chief avenger."[9] In her critique of substitutionary atonement, Delores Williams writes that "it seems more intelligent and more scriptural to understand that redemption had to do with God, through Jesus, giving humankind new vision to see the resources for positive, abundant relational life." In the gospel Jesus taught, she continues, "the kingdom of God is a metaphor of the hope God gives those attempting to right the relationship between self and self, between self and others, between self and God as prescribed in the sermon on the mount, in the golden rule and in the commandment to show love above all else."[10] In a similar shift of emphasis, Rosemary Radford Ruether writes that Jesus's principal purpose was not "to suffer and die." Rather, "redemption happens through resistance to the sway of evil, and in the experiences of conversion and healing by which communities of well-being are created."[11]

These ideas are consistent with the Latter-day Saint picture of a plan of happiness presented to and accepted by us in order that we could become joint-heirs with Christ. The focus of that proposal was the resurrection of Christ to bring life (resurrection) and the more abundant life (in present life and culminating in immortality and eternal life). The distinction we are suggesting between earlier atonement theologies and Restoration conceptions of Christ's mission was made long ago by the theologian Abelard (of Héloïse and Abelard fame). He believed that Christ died on the cross "not to satisfy the demands of the Devil, but to awaken humanity to love."[12] He protested: "Indeed, how cruel and perverse it seems that [God] should require the blood of the innocent as the price of anything, or that it should in any way please Him that an innocent person should be slain—still less that God should hold the death of His Son in such acceptance that by it He should be reconciled with the whole world."[13] This same contrast emerged with the Reformation: resisting the developments of Protestant theology, "Erasmus based his spiritual vision on imitating the living Jesus; Luther, on faith in the crucified Christ."[14]

One danger of the latter emphasis, the crucified Christ, has been noted by scholars such as Joan Brown and Rebecca Parker: an Anselmian Christianity too fixated on the suffering and death of Christ upon the cross runs the risk of providing "a divine model of submission to victimization which can have dangerous consequences for those who are in abusive and oppressive situations." In their discussion of Anselm's satisfaction theory, Brown and Parker say they fear a view of justice demanding that wrongs should not be righted "but that wrongs should be punished." Such an image, they argue, has sustained a culture of abuse, and they believe that "until this image is shattered it will be almost impossible to create a just society."[15] "We need to say no," Carter Heyward agrees, "to a tradition of violent punishment and to a God who would crucify . . . an innocent brother in our place—rather than hang with us, struggle with us, and grieve with us. . . . Jesus's mission was not to die but to live."[16]

One prominent theologian suggested in personal correspondence that Christianity has a "big problem" with its historic use of "legal analogies with criminality" as a model for atonement theology, and she agrees that "healing" might be more apt as a key concept.[17] This concept of healing would mark not an innovation but a correction of Calvin's lamentable analogy of mankind to "a poor criminal with a rope around his neck."[18] It would return us to an early Christian emphasis on humanity as wounded and the Atonement as healing, as expressed by the fourth-century church father Gregory of Nazianzus: "What has not been assumed [taken upon Himself] has not been *healed*" (our emphasis).[19] Such an emphasis would also find greater harmony with Restoration teachings.

In the simplest restatement of the Original Plan conceived in premortal councils, Jesus summarized the purpose and end and final result of the entire cosmic project—to be whole, fully realized beings. "Be ye perfect" is a common translation, but we prefer that of the translator Kevin Wuest, which is closer to the reading of the Greek text: "Therefore, as for you, you shall be those who are complete in your character, even as your Father in heaven is complete in his being" (Matt. 5:48). We note two distinctive surprises in Wuest's rendering. First, he translates the verb as a simple, comforting future tense, not an intimidating command form: you *will* (in the future) be.[20] Second, Wuest renders the Greek *teleios* as "complete." *Teleios*, completeness, takes us even closer to that original scene in premortal realms, that commencement of each individual saga, when Heavenly Parents proposed giving us the "privilege to advance like [Themselves] and be exalted with [Them]."[21] A *telos* is an envisioned end, finality, or completion of an intention or process. *Teleios* therefore signifies the fruition of a seed that has successfully come into bloom. One could see

Christ's words, on this occasion, as reassurance: Follow the precepts I have just laid down, and all will be well. You will find yourself a fully realized child of God. Or as Kevin Wuest renders the term *teleios*, "All is accomplished, their probation, their righteousness, God's purposes respecting them." One has "grow[n] into maturity of godliness."[22]

As we saw in Wiman's phrasing, we are "not corrupt, . . . but unfinished."[23] Elsewhere, Wuest writes that in the New Testament, "salvation . . . is growth in Christ-likeness."[24] To be whole, complete, and perfect in character and body alike, all this is implied in the Greek term employed in the Sermon on the Mount. In the Original Story, we are gods in embryo, and *healing* from life's wounds restores us to that path of growth. Salvation is *growth, process, unfolding of a potential.*

We can actually witness the tension between these two versions of Christ's atoning work—saving from sin versus healing from woundedness—in a textual contrast between two of the most important Bible translations in Christian history and the different ways they translate the Greek term *sodzo* ("heal" or "save"). Few biblical texts should be more central to our understanding of the Christian message as Jesus taught it than a record of one of the first public sermons delivered by the Apostle Peter. Second in sequence only to his Pentecostal testimony, this two-part address occurs before a Jewish crowd and then before a Jewish council. In the third chapter of Acts, in the King James Version, Peter heals "a certain man lame from his mother's womb" (Acts 3:2). An audience gathers, and after *enacting* the central principle of Jesus's ministry—healing—Peter uses the occasion, and his healed, restored teaching aid, to *emphasize* that central principle.

The first translation into English of these passages is by John Wycliffe, in the fourteenth century. Working *before* the Reformation, he rendered the critical verses into English as follows: "This [sick] man is made *saaf,*" "In the name of Jhesu Crist

. . . this man stondith *hool* bifor you;" There is no other name "in which it bihoveth us to be maad *saaf*" (Acts 4:9, 10, 12, our emphasis). The Middle English word *saaf*, like a principal meaning of the original Greek term *sodzo*, means "healed," "made whole."[25] In sum, Jesus Christ is the name and power whereby we can all be made whole, healed, sound, and complete. As was the design from the beginning—explained after Eve's fateful ascent, reaffirmed by Jesus on the Mount, and prophesied by the angel to Nephi—we would not be left "wounded" but would be restored to the path of divine ascent by Him who comes "with healing in his wings" (Mal. 4:2). The Healer and the Restorer to At-one-ment—the one who brings us into the fullest possible unity with each other and with the Heavenly Family—are the same. Even Augustine at one time saw our predicament in these terms; "through grace," he wrote, "the soul is healed from the wound of sin."[26]

A representative distortion from this blueprint is plain to see, dated to a text and time in history. When William Tyndale (upon whose work the King James Bible is based) translates this story of the healing of the paralytic, he forges in immutable form a narrative that is a stark departure from the original. He begins in Wycliffe's steps. This "impotent man . . . is made *whole*," he translates. "By the name of Jesus Christ . . . doth his man stand here before you *whole*," he continues. Then the fatal pivot on which the whole contemporary Christian message is built: "Neither is there *salvation* in any other; for there is none other name under heaven given whereby we must be *saved*." The story of healing a particular man, as a type of the healing of which we all stand in need, is shifted to a story about salvation from damnation. One Protestant commentator has conceded that "'salvation' means to rescue or protect, *although it also has the association of healing* or restoring to health" (our emphasis).[27] Our point is that in this story, context and language alike could not be clearer. Christ's incomparable gift is his power and desire to heal us all as individuals, regardless of the nature of our wounds. This is at-one-ment. Tragically, catastrophically, the preoccupation of Tyndale and his fellow Reformers with *sin* rather than *woundedness*, and *with salvation from hell* rather than *healing* from the "*infirmities*" and "*the pains of all*" triumphs (Alma 7:12; 2 Ne. 9:2).

Tyndale's biographer notes that by the time Tyndale translated the New Testament he had studied and "been deeply stirred" by Luther's exposition of original sin and depravity and that much of Tyndale's New Testament work is essentially an "expansion" of Luther.[28] Damnation is our default condition, that Reformer had taught. Tyndale accepted this premise that "by nature men are convicted to eternal damnation" and that we can be rescued only by Christ's imputed righteousness.[29] Tyndale's views, reflected in his translation, "smell strongly of Luther: the vivid image of the man bound to a post by a hundred thousand chains."[30] No wonder that, unlike Wycliffe, Tyndale was perfectly comfortable preferring saving to healing in Peter's sermon, even though nothing in the events or words of that story justifies such a reading.

We see the shift in emphasis—*healing from woundedness* to *salvation from hell*—in other passages of the King James Version, some more egregious than others. For example, one finds in Mark, Matthew, and Luke—in five healing accounts—the *identical* Greek phrase, repeated five times: *he pistis sou sesoken se* (ἡ πίστις σου σέσωκέν σε). The phrase is translated in the King James Version, respectively: "thy faith hath made thee whole" (Matt. 9:22), "thy faith hath made thee whole" (Mark 5:34), "thy faith hath made thee whole" (Mark 10:52); however, in Luke we find "thy faith hath *saved* thee" (Luke 18:42) and again "thy faith hath *saved* thee" (Luke 7:50). Why did the translators change Wycliffe's "healed" (*saaf*) to "saved" in these last two instances? The grammar and vocabulary are identical in the five cases. And as such parallelism implies, the situations are parallel. In Matthew 9 and Mark 5, Jesus "heals," He "makes whole," the woman with the issue of blood. In Mark 10 and Luke 18, He gives a blind man his sight. And yet, incongruously, in Luke's case Tyndale translates the act of healing as an act of "saving." His choice is a good example of a general inclination to associate Christ's ministry with saving rather than healing—even though healing is the central activity of his ministry in the New Testament and the Book of Mormon alike.[31]

The story in Luke 7 of the woman "who loved much" should be particularly instructive to us. We find her anointing the feet of the Christ from an alabaster box of ointment. Her affliction? She is, Luke tells us, "a sinner." And yet, Jesus speaks to her the identical words he spoke to the blind and to the ailing woman in the stories of Matthew and Mark: ἡ πίστις σου σέσωκέν σε. "Thy faith hath *healed* thee. Thy trust in me has made you *whole*" is the only reasonable rendering. The clear contextual implication is that Christ does not see before him a sinner; he sees a woman wounded by her past. Julian of Norwich understood the import of such a moment: Christ "wills that we readily incline to his gracious touching, more enjoying his complete love than sorrowing in our own failings." And as "sin is unclean and hurtful, . . . he shall heal us full fair."[32] The Son of God is the healer of our wounds.

Why, in this case as in the scene in Acts, would the King James translators (starting with Tyndale) employ the word *saved* rather than the *healed* of Wycliffe?[33] The deviation from the expected word (healed) is exactly like the unwarranted change we saw in the book of Acts. There a paralytic is *healed*; he is *healed* by the power of Christ, and so, preaches Peter, must you all be—saved? Or in Luke 18, the blind man given his sight is "saved"? There seems to be a clear disposition on the part of the translators—and remember, these are Reformation translators breaking with the language of the fourteenth-century Wycliffe—to immediately go to sin as the default human condition in need of saving, rather than go to woundedness as the universal human condition in need of healing. This tendency is not speculation on our part:

William Tyndale explicitly defends his use of the sin/salvation over wounded/healed paradigm, and it is thoroughly Lutheran in its rationale: the woman who anoints Christ "saw herself clearly in the law, both in what danger she was in, and her cruel bondage under sin, her horrible damnation and also the fearful sentence and judgment of God upon sinners."[34] Tyndale could see only saving, not healing, at stake.

Our point is not that we are not sinners, or that we do not need, in some sense, salvation. Our point is that Christ's language and ministry clearly indicate that from His perspective, as the story of the "woman who loved much" clearly tells us, sinning is a type of woundedness, like blindness or illness or lameness; it is an infirmity, a brokenness. As Healer, He ministers to the entire range of our afflictions: psychological, emotional, physical, and spiritual. The story of the "sinful" woman in particular has incredible potential to shift the emphasis in our relationship to Christ, from that of sinner and Savior to one of wounded and Healer. Restoration scripture makes it clear that the maladies we suffer span the spectrum and that Christ's act of atoning was intended to heal across the wide range—"the pains of every living creature." Or, as Elder David Bednar teaches, the Atonement addresses "not just . . . our sins and iniquities—but also . . . our physical pains and anguish, our weaknesses and shortcomings, our fear and frustrations, our disappointments and discouragement, our regrets and remorse, our despair and desperation, the injustices and inequities we experience, and the emotional distresses that beset us."[35]

The damage wrought—to ourselves and to others—by what we call sin needs healing just as much as other forms of spiritual and emotional harm do. The most fruitful way of considering sin may not be to see it as an evil that leads to a hell from which we must be *saved* but rather as a wound that needs to be *healed*. Both the context and the identical grammar require one and only one rendering of Christ's words to the weeping woman, and they are instructive: "Daughter, your faith has *healed* you. Enter into a state of peace."

In recent decades biblical scholarship has begun to move an understanding of atonement in this same direction. Conventional interpreters of *atonement*'s roots have seen the word as indicating "to cover." Mary Douglas, however, notes that while the Hebrew root *k-p-r* can mean "to cover or recover," it has a more complex meaning: "to *repair* a hole, *cure* a sickness, *mend* a rift, *make good* a torn or broken covering. . . . Atonement does not mean covering a sin so as to hide it from the sight of God; it means making good an outer layer which has rotted or been pierced" (our emphases).[36] In other words, *atonement* means "to heal." Margaret Barker agrees that the Hebrew *k-p-r,* translated as "atone," "has to mean restore, re-create, or heal" and argues that for the Hebrews, atonement was "the rite of healing."[37]

This reading of the meaning of *atonement* is twice affirmed in the Book of Mormon. Nephi foresees the day that "the Son of Righteousness shall appear unto them [that . . . look forward unto Christ with steadfastness]; and he shall heal them" (2 Ne. 26:9). The fulfillment of his prophecy comes in 3 Nephi. There, the Son of God does indeed appear to the Nephite people, and He pleads with those who anticipated His coming in language that clearly evokes the scene of the woman who washed Jesus's feet with her tears: "Will ye not return unto me, and repent of your sins, and be converted, *that I may heal* you?" (3 Ne. 9:13; our emphasis). In this magnificent scene we witness the purpose and culmination of Christ's great designs for us. The resurrected Christ here links the final stages of His mission with our return through conversion and healing. The familiar formula—"repent and be saved"—is expanded and enriched to a vastly more encompassing project. The lame, the blind, and the infirm, the guilt-ridden and sin-laden, the spiritually hungry and emotionally wounded, the wandering soul and lonely pilgrim—all are swept up in the embrace of His desire—and capacity—to heal. "Have you any that are sick among you? Bring them hither. Have ye any that are . . . *afflicted in any manner*? Bring them hither and *I will heal them,* for I have compassion upon you; my bowels are filled with mercy" (3 Nephi 17:7; our emphasis).

Christ here echoes the voice of the prodigal son's father—and His own—"a father who asks no questions, wanting only to welcome his children home."[38] Eugene England believed the realization of such an unprompted love, such a disposition to "set aside" our offense, was precisely the "shock of eternal love" necessary to prompt our healing—and our forgiving of and reconciliation with others.[39] Christ, in His mercy, already "hath atoned for [our] sins" (D&C 29:1). Christ, setting our sins aside, loving us perfectly and understandingly in whatever condition He finds us, empowers us to do likewise and complete the cycle of at-one-ing, of perfect healing.

Heaven, as Joseph taught, is not a matter of reward or position or place but a particular kind of sociability. We saw previously that heaven is the absolute harmony of human relationships. Among Latter-day Saint distinctives, this concept looms large. Some writers have contrasted our emphasis on a sociable heaven with Christianity's "theocentric"—God-centered—preoccupation. Theologian Kenneth Kirk, for example, believed that the final purpose and "end of life is the vision of God."[40] God is the fixed star around which the saved will gather in an eternal beatific vision, to which all the mystics aspired. With that image in mind, many Christians were anxious lest any human attachment threaten to displace God as the center of the galaxy of our love.

In C. S. Lewis's account of his wife's death and the spiritual illumination it brought him at great cost, he concludes with a cryptic sentence about her last words: "She said not to me but to the chaplain, 'I am at peace with God.' She smiled, but not at me. *Poi si torno all' eterna fontana.*"[41] The Italian is a quotation from Dante, at the moment when his beloved Beatrice guides him to the summit of Paradise and into the Eternal Presence: "Then she turned back to the eternal fountain."[42] Beatrice was Dante's earthly love, who led him to a greater. In the Divine Presence, both forget each other in the light of the True Source. In Lewis's case, his words betoken reorientation, recognition, and loss. *She said, but not to me. She smiled, but not at me.* In other words, he is crushed by a paradigm he believes he needs to embrace: *Though my preoccupation is with the wife I am losing, her love for me disappears in the greater radiance of love for God.*

The fear of loving family or beloved more than God has long pervaded Christian culture. The Restoration reexamines this longstanding tradition. Jesus named love of God first in the hierarchy of heavenly commands, with love of others second (Matt. 22:38–39). Yet, when Enoch asks a weeping God the Father ("Man of Holiness") the cause of His tears, His answer has three astonishing dimensions. The first appears when God prefaces His response by reciting the two great commandments but which He here pronounces *in reverse order*: "Unto thy brethren have I said, and also given commandment, that they should love one another, and that they should choose me, their Father." The second paradigm disruption is that though God's children have clearly broken both commands, God's grief is over their violation of the second. He is not weeping because they have failed to worship, honor, or obey Him; "Behold, they are without affection, and they hate their own blood." Third, His tears flow, indeed, "the whole heavens shall weep over them . . . seeing these shall *suffer*." Human suffering, not human sin, is the focus of his grief. Three times the account affirms, and Enoch marvels, that God's weeping is over human "misery."

These verses are the clearest prism through which to see our Divine Parents' true nature and greatest concern. It is not for Themselves, for Their glory, or for Their priority in our hearts that They labor. Their greatest longing made manifest in those verses accords with the deepest desire *we* know as parents—or one day shall: that our children live in love and harmony with one another. That we would be jealous of our children's love for each other is simply perverse. Love in a community of perfect sociability is not competitive—it is mutually reinforcing. How could we have missed that lesson? To serve each other *is* to serve God. Ministering to each other *is* to honor and worship Them, as Benjamin taught. To succor the thirsty or to feed the hungry *is* to succor Christ, to feed Christ. We may make distinctions, but God does not. We cannot contribute to the heavenly community, the Zion of perfect sociability, if our relationships with each other are fractured. Another way of saying this is that our love for one another does not *compete* with our love for God—as C. S. Lewis and countless poets have suggested; our love for one another *registers* with God as love for Them; it is the most concrete manifestation of our love for God and the form of worship They most desire.

If this idea is true—as we believe Enoch attests—then the work of atonement would be intended to bring about the healing and unifying of the entire human family. In this project, we are invited to be coparticipants with the Godhead. Indeed, atonement cannot be accomplished without our collaboration. The most emphatic invitation to collaborate comes at that moment when we participate in the ordinance of adoption into the Heavenly Family—otherwise known as baptism. At this most appropriate moment of covenant making, we commit to join in the enterprise of Zion-building, to erect, edify, and constitute a community of love—of at-one-ment. Mosiah's language beautifully reminds us that we have been called to work collaboratively *with* the Godhead in Their healing enterprise.

At one time, converts to the restored faith vocally affirmed the baptismal covenants at water's edge. At the present, the covenants outlined in Mosiah 18:8–10 are implicit. We covenant to "bear one another's burdens, that they may be light." That language evokes the role of God the Christ, who bore our burdens throughout His life, into Gethsemane and onto Golgotha. We pledge to "mourn with those that mourn." These words call to mind that same God the Father who revealed to Enoch that He wept tears of grief, in solidarity with those who suffered misery and fratricidal hate. We can be assured, as Chieko Okazaki has written, that both our Heavenly Parents "have suffered with us . . . in our own suffering."[43] And we covenant to "comfort those that stand in need of comfort." That phrasing could hardly direct us more explicitly to the role of God the Holy Spirit, our Comforter in all our afflictions. Though we (sadly) no longer verbally pronounce the words of a baptismal covenant, remembering this sacred trilogy of obligation to mourn, to share burdens, and to comfort can make the at-one-ing of God's family a daily act of worship in which we participate with the Divine Family.

We believe one final shift is called for in our thinking about atonement. Oh, that we still pronounced *atonement* as it would have been heard in William Tyndale's pronunciation: at-one-ment! We would then learn two of its aspects we may have forgotten. First, that the purpose of Christ's work of healing was intended to restore unity to the human family and reunite us with God—at "oneness." All things tend toward the "great one-ing between Christ and us," Julian of Norwich wrote.[44] And second, Wycliffe's earlier rendering of *atonement* as "reconciliation" would call to mind a process that requires active effort by *both* parties. The Atonement is not something Christ performed. It is not adequately encompassed in a picture of a suffering Jesus in Gethsemane *or* the Christ nailed to the cross. Important as those events are, they no more capture the aspiration and reality of atonement than a wedding proposal captures the totality of a joyful and harmonious companionate marriage. The central, two-fold process of atonement is captured in the Healer's own words, "Draw near to God and he will draw near to you" (James 4:8). The most fitting image of atonement is that given us in the book of Moses: "And the Lord said unto Enoch: Then shalt thou and all thy city meet them there, and we will receive them into our bosom, and they shall see us; and we will fall upon their necks, and they shall fall upon our necks, and we will kiss each other; And there shall be mine abode, and it shall be Zion" (Moses 7:63–64).

This passage is stunningly new, unexpected, and unlike the depictions over the centuries of losing ourselves in the beatific vision. Contrary to the fears of C. S. Lewis, we find here no diminution of earthly bonds, eclipsed in a superior Divine Presence. Here is totality, wholeness, reunion, healing, and unity. "They [the heavenly community] shall see *us!*" God and Christ, the living and the departed, divine and human, all merge into one celebratory community of the holy. That is the picture of atonement, reconciliation, "oneing," brought to its perfect fulfillment.

This picture may be too distant, too abstract for those of us in immediate pain, however. We might ask, How does Christ's atoning endeavor actually heal me, repair me and my relationships, make me one with myself and with Him, *in the here and now*? It would be marvelous if Alma's experience were the pattern for us all: angelic visitation; acute sense of woundedness and need; despair crescendoing in the desperate plea, "O Jesus . . . have mercy on me"; followed by immediate "joy" and "marvelous light" (Alma 36:18–20). More commonly, healing begins gradually when we first open ourselves to the possibility that we are already in the embrace of a love greater than any we have known. Even those who doubt can begin by considering the remarkable, yet historical, fact of a young, itinerant Galilean rabbi who two thousand years ago offered himself up to barbaric execution as a criminal. He endured unspeakable pain, because by so doing He was offering me, personally, respite from the pains and humiliations and failures and wounds of my life, whether inflicted by others or by my own foolish choices. As the Book of Mormon testified would happen, we have found ourselves "drawn" to this person of unfathomable kindness and compassion (3 Ne. 27:14).

We need to provide a way for Christ to affirm that He knows us by name, that He has in reality set His heart upon us. That may take the form of pondering those words that most resonate with our heartstrings: Jesus's expression of love for His disciples ("Little children, yet a little while I am with you . . . I go to prepare a place for you"), the testimony of John ("God sent his son into the world not to condemn us, but to heal us"), Dostoevsky's witness of Christ that emerged through his own "great crucible of doubt" ("Believe that nothing is more beautiful, profound, sympathetic, reasonable, . . . and more powerful than Christ"), or the lyrics to Dustin Kensrue's "Please Come Home" ("Please come home, please come home / Don't you know that I still love you? / And I don't care where you've been").[45] We must find a medium through which God can speak to us. We need to find our own Urim and Thummim.

In some cases, the healing will come slowly or incompletely. However, in such cases, our own experience of unmet need is a witness to the fact that Christ's work of redemptive healing relies upon us as collaborators in His ministry of at-one-ing. "God will wipe away all tears from off all faces" (Isa. 25:8). The promise is given, but the timetable is not. The urgent responsibility to minister to the wounded is upon us all. Our baptismal covenants are the operative way by which Christ's atoning ministry becomes universal.

NOTES

1   Stephen Finlan, *Problems with Atonement: The Origins of, and Controversy about, the Atonement Doctrine* (Collegeville, MN: Liturgical Press, 2005), 84. Finlan is here citing Jack Nelson-Pallmeyer, *Jesus Against Christianity* (Harrisburg: Trinity, 2001), 222–24.

2   Finlan, *Problems with Atonement*, 104.

3   Gregory of Nyssa (as recast by Rufinus of Aquileia), in Henry Bettenson, ed., *Documents of the Christian Church* (Oxford: Oxford University Press, 1967), 34.

4   Anselm, *Cur deus homo?* 1:xi–xiii, in Henry Bettenson, ed., *Documents of the Christian Church* (New York: Oxford University Press, 1947), 196–97.

5   John Calvin, "Reply to Sadoleto," in John C. Olin, ed., *A Reformation Debate* (Grand Rapids, MI: Baker, 2002), 66.

6   Martin Luther, *Commentary on the Galatians* (Lafayette, IN: Sovereign Grace, 2001), 274.

7   David Daniell, *William Tyndale: A Biography* (New Haven: Yale University Press, 1994), 131.

8   René Gerard, *Things Hidden Since the Foundation of the World* (Stanford: Stanford University Press, 1987), 182.

9   J. Denny Weaver, "Violence in Christian Theology," *Cross Currents* 51, no. 2 (Summer 2001): 150–76.

10   Delores Williams, *Sisters in the Wilderness: The Challenge of Womanist God-Talk* (Maryknoll, NY: Orbis, 1993), 166. Cited in J. Denny Weaver, *The Nonviolent Atonement* (Grand Rapids, MI: Eerdmans, 2001), 165.

11   Rosemary Radford Ruether, *Introducing Redemption in Christian Feminism* (Sheffield, UK: Sheffield Academic Press, 1998), 104–105. Cited in Weaver, *Nonviolent Atonement*, 125.

12   The paraphrase of Abelard is by Tom Holland, *Dominion: How the Christian Revolution Remade the World* (New York: Basic Books, 2019), 245.

13   Quoted in Diana Butler Bass, *A People's History of Christianity* (New York: HarperCollins, 1989), 115–16.

14   Michael Massing, *Fatal Discord: Erasmus, Luther, and the Fight for the Western Mind* (New York: HarperCollins, 2018), 240.

15   Joanne Carlos Brown and Rebecca Parker, "For God So Loved the World?" in *Christianity, Patriarchy, and Abuse: A Feminist Critique*, ed. Joanne Carlson Brown and Carole R. Bohn (New York: Pilgrim Press, 1989), 7–9.

Cited in J. Denny Weaver, *The Nonviolent Atonement* (Grand Rapids, MI: Eerdmans, 2001), 127–29.

16 Carter Heyward, *Saving Jesus from Those Who Are Right: Rethinking What It Means to Be Christian* (Minneapolis: Fortress Press, 1999), 175, 138. In Weaver, *Nonviolent Atonement*, 152–53.

17 Frances Young, personal correspondence with Andrew Teal, November 5, 2019, in reference to our own recasting of *sodzo* as "healing" rather than "saving."

18 John Calvin, *Sermons on Genesis 1–11*, trans. Rob Roy MacGregor (East Peoria, IL: Banner of Truth Trust, 2009), 260.

19 ; Gregory of Nazianzus, *Letter* 101.32, in *Nicene and Post-Nicene Fathers*, 2nd series (Peabody, MA: Hendrickson, 1994), 7:440.

20 The verb is in fact a future indicative, though a future indicative can on occasion be rendered as an imperative. We agree with those (few) translators who prefer the simple future to the command. As one Greek scholar explained, "The passage contains plenty of imperatives (not jussive futures), where imperatives are wanted (e.g., at 5.44 ἀγαπᾶτε, προσεύχεσθε, ποιεῖτε) and plenty of future indicatives that are quite clearly to be understood as future indicatives and not as jussives. Note, too, that at 5.44 the present imperative ἀγαπᾶτε *replaces* the jussive future of the direct quote! Clearly Jesus himself prefers imperatives when he wants to issue a direct order." Julie Laskaris, personal communication with author, November 4, 2019.

21 Stan Larson, "The King Follett Discourse: A Newly Amalgamated Text," *BYU Studies* 18, no. 2 (Winter 1978): 204.

22 Kenneth S. Wuest, *Wuest's Word Studies from the Greek New Testament* (Grand Rapids, MI: Eerdmans, 1973), *Treasures* section, 3:120, 117.

23 Christian Wiman, *My Bright Abyss* (New York: Farrar, Straus and Giroux, 2014), 103.

24 Wuest, *Word Studies*, *Golden Nuggets* section, 3:70.

25 Walter W. Skeat, *Concise Dictionary of Middle English From A.D. 1150 to 1580* (self-pub., 2020), s.v. "saaf."

26 Augustine, *Spir. et litt.* 30.52. Cited in Stuart Squires, *Pelagian Controversy: An Introduction to the Enemies of Grace and the Conspiracy of Lost Souls* (Eugene OR: Pickwick, 2019), 208.

27 Robert Sherman, *King, Priest, Prophet: A Trinitarian Theology of Atonement* (London: T&T Clark, 2004), 15.

28 David Daniell, *William Tyndale: A Biography* (New Haven, CT: Yale University Press, 1994), 30, 161.

29 Daniell, *Tyndale*, 124.

30 Daniell, *Tyndale*, 132.

31 See in the latter instance, 1 Nephi 11:28.

32 Denise N. Baker, ed., *The Showings of Julian of Norwich* 16.81 and 14.63 and (New York: Norton, 2005), pp. 121, 98. We have modernized the spelling and at times modified the translation.

33 Wycliffe's word is *saaf*, "healed" or "made whole."

34 Daniell, *Tyndale*, 165.

35 Elder David A. Bednar, "Bear Up Their Burdens with Ease" *Ensign* 44, no. 5 (May 2014): 89–90.

36 Mary Douglas, "Atonement in Leviticus," *Jewish Studies Quarterly*, no. 1 (1993–94): 117–18.

37 Margaret Barker, "Atonement: The Rite of Healing" (paper presented to the Society for Old Testament Study in Edinburgh, July 1994); published in *Scottish Journal of Theology* 49, no.1 (February 1996): 1–20. The Douglas citation in note 34 above is quoted by Barker.

38 Henri J. M. Nouwen, *The Return of the Prodigal Son: A Story of Homecoming* (New York: Doubleday, 1994), 23.

39 Eugene England, "That They Might Not Suffer: The Gift of Atonement," *Dialogue* 1, no. 3 (Autumn 1966): 141–55.

40 Kenneth Kirk, *The Vision of God: The Christian Doctrine of the Summum Bonum* (New York: Harper, 1932), ix.

41 C. S. Lewis, *A Grief Observed* (New York: HarperOne, 2001), 75.

42 Dante, *Paradiso* 31.93, trans. John Ciardi (New York: New American Library, 1970), 341.

43 Chieko N. Okazaki, *Sanctuary* (Salt Lake City: Deseret, 1997), 149.

44 Baker, *Showings of Julian of Norwich*, 8.18, p. 30.

45 John 13:33, 14:2; John 3:17, our translation; Joseph Frank, *Dostoevsky: The Years of Ordeal, 1850–1859* (Princeton: Princeton University Press, 1987), 160; Dustin Kensrue, "Please Come Home," *Please Come Home* (Equal Vision, 2007).

CHAPTER FOURTEEN

Grace

From Declaring Righteous to Becoming Righteous

N o word in the Christian religious vocabulary is the source of more contention, misunderstanding, and misdirection than *grace*. Let us first make sure we understand what grace means to many of our Christian friends, and what it cannot mean if we accept the premises of the Restoration. We saw in chapter 2 that Augustine rewrote Christian theology in accordance with his belief that through faith we are justified. He took *justification* to mean "the declaring of someone to be righteous: God 'imputes' the merits of the crucified and risen Christ through grace to a fallen human being, who remains without inherent merit."[1] This idea of grace as a gift of righteousness that is "imputed" to us becomes the nucleus of the Reformation spearheaded by Luther. We are "saved" by faith, meaning we trust that Christ is perfectly reliable, and since we are judged by His perfect righteousness standing in place of our own sinfulness, we are held guiltless. With Him standing effectively in our stead at judgment, we are considered righteous.

"Considered" blameless is the key. Protestants believe that Christ does not just suffer in our stead; He is judged in our stead. Hence one is justified in God's judgment though one is actually "wholly a sinner," in Luther's famous language (*"simul justus et peccator"*).[2] Or as the Thirty-nine Articles (the creedal basis of most

Protestant denominations) state, "We are accounted righteous before God, only for the merit of our Lord and Saviour Jesus Christ by Faith" (Article 11). Reformation historian Diarmaid MacCulloch elaborates: "There was no human merit, not even among the elect. . . . All righteousness in a humanity which was utterly fallen and under destruction was that of Christ himself: an alien righteousness given to humanity by grace. Human beings could never actually *be* 'just' or righteous" (our emphasis).[3]

This teaching sounds very much like Zeezrom's claim, rather harshly condemned in the Book of Mormon, that God will "save his people *in* their sins" (Alma 11:34, our emphasis). It is hard to imagine what such a conception would even mean for God's nature or purposes or for such a stunted human potential. As Latter-day Saints understand the principle, salvation is the gradual development of each and every being into "a just and holy being," as Joseph taught.[4] It is a long process of learning how to participate in "the divine nature," as Peter foresaw (2 Pet. 1:4). It is simply not in God's power to gift us with a holy character or magically insert us into healthy relationality. As Joseph taught from the *Lectures on Theology* (better known as the *Lectures on Faith*), "Why purify [themselves] as he is pure? Because, if they do not they cannot be like him."[5] In Augustine's own day, alarmed Christians saw the dangerous road to which his innovations regarding grace would lead: his teachings threatened to "undermine the whole foundation of the Christian life as an active and loving co-operation between God and man."[6] That threat became institutionalized in normative Christianity.

Joseph explained why righteousness cannot be imputed, why God's grace cannot short-circuit the process of sanctification: Only "that which is governed by law is also preserved by law and perfected and sanctified by the same. That which breaketh a law, and abideth not by law . . . cannot be sanctified by . . . mercy," that is, by grace (D&C 88:35). The great mystic Emmanuel

Swedenborg understood law in the same way: "Man is so created that he can be more and more closely united to the Lord. He is so united not by knowledge alone, nor by intelligence alone, nor even by wisdom alone, but by a life in accordance with these."[7] The "life in accordance" will be a long and gradual process as we acquire and practice greater knowledge, intelligence, and wisdom.

This is an empowering definition of *law*: those precepts that train us in the nature of happiness and therefore in the nature of godliness. They are the principles by which, in Joseph's language, assisted by the Holy Spirit, we become pure and holy. *Law* refers to the articulation of certain realities inherent in the texture of the universe, realities that link certain choices to what is sweet and others to what is bitter, some that unify us and some that fracture community. Laws are given to tutor us in holy conduct that becomes holy character. That is why only "he who is . . . able to abide the law of a celestial kingdom can . . . abide a celestial glory" (D&C 88:34–35, 25). Or as Brigham Young put the case, "It being the will and design of the Father, Son, and Holy Ghost . . . that you should be a Saint, will not make you one, contrary to your own choice."[8] Seeing law in such a light, we understand why Ezra Taft Benson counseled that "when obedience ceases to be an irritant and becomes our quest, in that moment God will endow us with power."[9]

In other words, contra the whole Protestant heritage, with its foundation in *sola gratia* (salvation by grace alone) and the doctrine of imputed righteousness, Saints proclaim that "with all eternity before them for the exercise of every power with which the Creator endowed them, spiritual, mental and physical," they can be "perfected by experience and obedience to eternal law, and ready to act in harmony with celestial intelligences."[10] In light of Latter-day Saint conceptions of the human spirit as being inherently divine, we are promised full divinity as we practice the essence of that divine principle most beautifully articulated in the three baptismal covenants. Luther's dictum that "we are justified by God's judgment though wholly a sinner" is sadly defeatist and negates the transformative—and cooperative—power of Christ's Atonement, which eventuates in the immortality and eternal life of the entire human family.

And yet, Nephi taught that we are indeed "saved by grace, after all that we can do" (2 Ne. 25:23). As Saints we should have no problem acknowledging the abundant "giftedness" that everywhere colors the Great Plan of Happiness from beginning to end. First, because Christ's gift precedes rather than follows our need. Creation anticipates our arrival, His Atonement foresees our sorrows and suffering, and His Resurrection inaugurates our own. And second, because "Jesus had not finished his work when his body was slain, neither did he finish it after his resurrection from the dead; although he had accomplished the purpose for which he then came to the earth, he had not fulfilled all his work. And when will he? Not until he has redeemed and saved every son and daughter of our father Adam that have been or ever will be born upon this earth to the end of time."[11] Could this be what Christ meant, when He said of his travails in Gethsemane, "And I partook and finished my *preparations* unto the children of men" (D&C 19:19, our emphasis)?[12]

We trust that as myriad agents, here and across the veil, strengthen and support and encourage us, so do the tendrils of Christ's love succor and strengthen, in myriad ways tangible though unrecognized. As Brigham Young suggested, "When we obtain celestial glory we shall have to explain that it is through the grace of God after all."[13] Grace describes every aspect of our relationship and interaction with the Healing One because that relationship is not transactional. His love precedes and transcends any action, merit, or fault of ours. "He first loved us" (1 John 4:19). We believe that God's love for us is a love that is wholly uncontaminated by preconditions, or by expectations. It is nowhere

more beautifully illustrated than in a dream vision that Truman
Madsen described:

> We had just come from a parched visit to Egypt and the
> Sinai desert. There, even the native Bedouin can survive
> in the sweltering heat no more than three hours without
> water. We had reminded our students of one of the few
> self-regarding cries of the Savior from the cross: "I thirst,"
> to which the response was a sponge of vinegar. That night
> I had a dream. I was beaten down on my hands and knees
> and was conscious of a burning thirst. As I lifted to my lips
> a small cup of liquid, an unearthly liquid—cool, radiant,
> delicious—I felt a pair of compassionate hands behind me
> but not touching. Their very presence near my head and neck
> created a comfortable, blessed feeling. And then the miracle.
> As I drank in exquisite relief, the cup filled continually to the
> top. The more I sought to quench my whole-souled thirst,
> the more it filled and flowed. A wave of gratitude to Christ
> (for in the dream the Comforter was Christ) consumed
> me, and the impulse was to stop drinking and turn around
> to thank him. But by his subtle power the sweet assurance
> came that my drinking was his thanks; it was what he most
> wanted; it was his reward, even his glory. It was like the
> gracious hostess who takes great delight in seeing her family
> and guests eat heartily. I knew, and I knew he knew. So I
> drank and drank until I was full. Only then was he gone.[14]

NOTES

1   Diarmaid MacCulloch, *The Reformation: A History* (New York: Viking, 2004), 115.

2   Quoted in Paul Althaus, *The Theology of Martin Luther*, trans. Robert C. Schultz (Philadelphia: Fortress, 1966), 242. See, for commentary and discussion of the principle, the essays in Wayne Stumme, *The Gospel of Justification in Christ: Where Does the Church Stand Today?* (Grand Rapids: Eerdmans, 2006).

3   Diarmaid MacCulloch, *Thomas Cranmer: A Life* (New Haven: Yale University Press, 1996), 345.

4   Theology Lecture Seventh, 1835 D&C, 66–67.

5   1 John 3:2–3; Theology Lecture Seventh, 1835 D&C, 66–67.

6   B. R. Rees, *Life*, in *Pelagius: Life and Letters* (Woodbridge, UK: Boydell, 1991), 128.

7   Julian Smyth and William Wunsch, *The Gist of Swedenborg* (New York: Swedenborg Foundation, 1920), 12.

8   Richard S. Van Wagoner, ed., *Complete Discourses of Brigham Young* (Salt Lake City: Smith-Petit Foundation, 2009), 3:1378.

9   Quoted in Donald Staheli, "Obedience—Life's Great Challenge," *Ensign* 28, no. 5 (May 1998): 82.

10   Charles W. Penrose, *Mormon Doctrine, Plain and Simple: Or Leaves from the Tree of Life* (Salt Lake City: Juvenile Instructor, 1888), 49.

11   Joseph F. Smith, in *Journal of Discourses,* 19:264. He excepted "sons of perdition," but we note that D&C 76:45 indicates that "no man knows" their ultimate fate.

12   We thank Susan Griffith for this insight.

13   Richard S. Van Wagoner, ed., *Complete Discourses of Brigham Young* (Salt Lake City: Smith-Petit Foundation, 2009), 1:276.

14   Truman G. Madsen, "The Savior, the Sacrament, and Self-Worth," in *The Arms of His Love: Talks from the 1999 Women's Conference* (Salt Lake City: Deseret, 2000), 253.

CHAPTER FIFTEEN

Worthiness
From Merit to Miracle

Retaining this collaborative vision of "an active and loving co-operation between God and man" can rescue us from the pitfalls associated with that frightful word, *worthiness*. A little history may illustrate the term's dangers. Jesus espoused an ethic of virtue, holiness, cleanliness. The pure in heart, He said, would see God. (Matt. 5:8). It seemed logical to early Christians to institute norms, rules of behavior, and codes of conduct that would assist us in achieving that end. This institutionalization results almost inevitably in the foregrounding in the disciple's life of a kind of formalism. Kenneth Kirk notes that already in the early Christian centuries, the litmus test of rules "push[ed] their way more and more into the foreground of the code, and obedience and conformity [took] the place of enthusiastic loyalty as the basis of Christian life."[1] The sad effect of this development is a kind of self-concern, a self-consciousness, that thwarts the outward-looking charity that is the disciple's true calling. "Communion with God, present and future, is relegated to the background; salvation and recompense become the main objects of the Christian's desire."[2]

What began as an admirable desire to abide by the precepts of the Master, which are other-oriented, all too easily morphed into an obsession with one's own spiritual athleticism. No one is a beneficiary in such a case: not the individual, not God, and certainly not one's neighbors. Some early Christians went to absurd lengths to demonstrate their mastery of self-discipline: Simeon Stylites, a renowned ascetic of the fifth century, lived for thirty-seven years on a small platform atop a pillar in Syria—and hundreds followed his example. Tens of thousands of Christians lived monastic lives of seclusion and rigorous self-deprivation. Those known as anchorites had themselves entombed while alive to ensure an escape-proof life of reflection. And today, many modern Saints carefully monitor their performance and mark their achievements with awards and merit badges. This is not to devalue the virtues of discipline. Undoubtedly, mastery of self enables us to be more effective vehicles for God's purposes. However, two tragedies ensue from this orientation that makes personal spirituality the supreme achievement. It short-circuits God's purposes and priorities. And it can only lead to misery.

Any path to spirituality that focuses on the self and its relationship to God misconstrues what the Restoration teaches about the two great commandments: they are inseparably intertwined, as we saw in God's lament to Enoch. One theologian writes that "the highest prerogative of the Christian, in this life as well as hereafter, is the activity of *worship*."[3] As King Benjamin taught, however, we can worship God only *by* devoting ourselves to the service of our sisters and brothers. We love God, and we serve God, *by* ministering to His children—all of whom are our kin. It is not our own spiritual performance, but our devotion to those around us, that is the point of Restoration teachings. God is not ever assessing our worthiness; They are concerned that we collaborate with Them to the best of our abilities in bringing peace and healing, the abundant life and eternal life, to the human family. We cannot serve God separate and apart from actively loving His children. William Tyndale got this point right: "A Christian worketh to make his weak brother perfecter and not to seek a higher place in heaven."[4] One of the most beautiful of Brigham Young's preachings evinced the freedom that comes when we escape the trap of perpetually gauging our own worthiness:

> Others say, where is my crown, where is my increase, where is my glory, and [they are] looking after pay all the time. I say, "Look after your duty; seek to know it and do it, and it's all right about your pay." . . . I'll risk it if some are afraid . . . that they will come short of going into the celestial kingdom, and they wonder if they will be saved with the sanctified. I don't care anything about it. I have enlisted in the service of my God and will leave it to him what he'll do with me.[5]

Our preoccupation with worthiness on that score is not only misdirected but also the source of the epidemic of guilt that afflicts the body of Christ. How might we find a way of confronting our own life and actions that does not lead to inevitable feelings of inadequacy, failure, and disappointment in self? Other Christians frequently describe salvation in terms of worthiness, or acceptance. A major figure in the New Perspective on Paul movement—which is radically reevaluating Protestant readings of Paul—begins his book on the subject by addressing the question of what we must do to win "God's acceptance" and cites another scholar who is also asking about the respective options of faith or works to "win God's favor."[6]

Such a vision of God is appalling. These scholars are invoking a sovereign deity who holds His love in reserve, waiting upon our fealty and proof of merit. God has never predicated Their relationship with us on our "worthiness." As Martin Luther King wrote, "There is no graded scale of essential worth."[7] That is why the loving destiny that awaits us, Elder Uchtdorf affirmed, is not a prize won "with the currency of obedience."[8] Would we want to be part of a marriage, or a friendship, in which love is transactional, based on the kind of reciprocity that so confounded Job? Love worth having is not love that is earned; our worth is not God's cup to be filled with correct words and gestures and deeds. Our worth already has the greatest validation of which the cosmos is capable. The universe's most perfect and holy Being came to heal us from our wounds, redeem us from death, and shepherd us into immortality and life eternal. That was Christ's testament to our worth(iness), and no force on earth or in hell can impugn a worth so powerfully affirmed.

God's love, Their commitment to us, *precedes* any action on our part. When Jesus looked upon the rich young man, "beholding him, [he] loved him" (Mark 10:21). The sequence tells us everything: Jesus beheld him, and He loved him, *before* the young man decided to follow, or not to follow, the Lord— and independently of whatever decision he was yet to make. In Zenos's allegory of the vineyard, the Lord nourishes his wild olive trees *twenty-two times*. Twenty-two times He persists in lovingly tending, pruning, cultivating, caring for, and lavishing love and care and effort on one single tree, a wild tree, that to all appearances is unresponsive to His efforts. As with us, His love *precedes* the coming of any fruit.

We believe it is a slander against God to presume that Their compassion is measured to our merit. The story of the prodigal son tells us otherwise. As Henri Nouwen writes, "I have come to know in a small way what it means to be a father who asks no questions, wanting only to welcome his children home."[9] We are all prodigals, we have all wandered, and we all fall short of our potential—without exception. And yet, as David Bentley Hart writes, "The character of even the very worst among us is in part the product of external contingencies, and somewhere in the history of every soul there are moments when a better way was missed by mischance, or by malign interventions from without, or by disorders of the mind within, rather than by intentional perversity on the soul's own part."[10] Our Heavenly Parents are more generous with us than we are with ourselves because They are wiser than we are. This is why we might best understand mercy not as turning a *blind eye* to our actions but as seeing them with a fully *understanding* eye.

As Nouwen reminds us, "Our brokenness has no other beauty but the beauty that comes from the compassion that surrounds it."[11] The love that envelops us is not based on our worthiness. It is not our merit that brings it forth. This love, unsolicited, is the miracle that tells us we have a permanent and cherished place in the universe. A friend wrote of the moment when from the depths of her own dark night of the soul, she experienced a blinding epiphany, a perfect realization of a God of absolute, nonjudgmental love:

> I thought of Christ as a condemning being who demanded blind following, or else packed you off to a burning abyss. I thought, if I were to feel anything, it would be the disgust of a being who had seen my whole life in detail, knew the mountain of things I had done "wrong" in his book and was repulsed. Instead, I felt something that will never leave me. My mind could not have manufactured it. If I could have invented something so beautiful, I would have done it a long time ago. I felt that everything about me and my life—every moment of grief, joy, heartache, trauma and darkness—was all perfectly understood and none of it was condemned. I didn't feel guilted, shamed or rejected. I felt loved. Not in the watery way society often uses the word. It was deep as an ocean. It was rich as cream. It was without bounds or conditions.[12]

Perhaps, if we listen, we can hear the Healer's words as the poet Alfred Tennyson did, consumed as he was by his own feelings of unworthiness:

Thou canst not move me from thy side,

Nor human frailty do me wrong. . . .

So fret not, . . .

That life is dashed with flecks of sin.

Abide. Thy wealth is gathered in,

When time hath sundered shell from pearl.[13]

NOTES

1   Kenneth Kirk, *The Vision of God: The Christian Doctrine of the Summum Bonum* (New York: Harper, 1932), 133.

2   Kirk, *Vision of God*, 138.

3   Kirk, *Vision of God*, xvii.

4   David Daniell, *William Tyndale: A Biography* (New Haven, CT: Yale University Press, 1994), 377.

5   Richard S. Van Wagoner, ed., *Complete Discourses of Brigham Young* (Salt Lake City: Smith-Petit Foundation, 2009), 1:282.

6   James D. G. Dunn, *The New Perspective on Paul*, rev. ed. (Grand Rapids: Eerdmans 2005), 1.

7   Martin Luther King, *Where Do We Go from Here: Chaos or Community?* (Boston: Beacon Press, 2010), 97, cited in Tom Holland, *Dominion: How the Christian Revolution Remade the World* (New York: Basic Books, 2019), 494.

8   Dieter F. Uchtdorf, "O How Great the Plan of Our God!," *Ensign* 46, no. 11 (November 2016): 21.

9   Henri J. M. Nouwen, *Return of the Prodigal Son: A Story of Homecoming* (New York: Doubleday, 1994), 22–23.

10   David Bentley Hart, *That All Shall Be Saved: Heaven, Hell, and Universal Salvation* (New Haven: Yale University Press, 2019), 39.

11   Nouwen, *Return of the Prodigal*, 35.

12   Personal correspondence with authors, August 9, 2020.

13   Alfred Tennyson, "In Memoriam," in *The Works of Alfred Lord Tennyson* (London: Macmillan, 1907), 260.

CHAPTER SIXTEEN

Judgment

From Court to Waystation

But what of judgment? What of the assignment of guilt and punishment? That some judgment will take place is beyond dispute—the scriptures are too emphatic to deny the inevitability of some phase of our eternal journey, following this one, to which the name "judgment" is applied. The question is, *what* function does that judgment have? In some Christian faith traditions, the judgment is rather like a criminal proceeding, the purpose of which is the assessment of guilt or innocence followed by the designation of the appropriate reward or punishment. The Catholic dogma holds that "immediately after death the eternal destiny of each separated soul is decided by the just judgment of God." Following this process, "souls that are perfectly pure are at once admitted to the beatific vision of the Godhead (*ipsum Deum unum et trinum*), and those who depart in actual mortal sin, or merely with original sin, are at once consigned to eternal punishment."[1] Calvin anticipated that on Judgment Day, God will require us to "recount those evil deeds like criminals before a judge with his record and his clerk—so when God examines us that way, it is as if we see him in a visible way with his records, his witnesses, and his instructions all ready to condemn us."[2] Some defendants God has preselected for salvation through grace alone; most others will be consigned to hell. Or, as Michael the demon explains in *The Good Place*, "The premise of our system is that a person's score during her time on earth is final and unarguable."[3] (That is not a scenario any more pleasant to contemplate than that of angelic scorekeepers who are "silent notes taking of every action!")[4]

As a matter of historical fact, the Reformation effected changes in our religious experience that worked to emphasize the terrors of damnation and judgment, foment guilt, and alienate us from the love of God. In one of their principal innovations, Reformers intended to make the Communion—what we call the Sacrament—"the centre-piece of the regular weekly worship of the Church." To their surprise, however, their designs failed: "People did not want to make their communion on such a frequent basis." The explanation was not hard to find. The ancient language of the mass had included the words "that the [emblems] should preserve their bodies and souls to everlasting life." (Ignatius, one of the earliest Christian writers, called the Eucharist "the medicine of immortality.")[5] Communicants of the new rites were instead called to a new focus: "Think of the sacrifice of Christ on the cross." Pondering the extent of the Lord's sacrifice is commendable, but it is all a question of emphasis and purpose. "The fierce exhortations to self-examination" made parishioners feel "that they were not worthy to receive" the emblems. A somber but joy-filled celebration of Christ's gift was overwhelmed by a depressing absorption in one's own unworthiness—and attendance plummeted accordingly.[6]

Fear of judgment has been exacerbated by the historically universal belief that "the moment of death is the end of our pilgrimage, the end of our status" as someone on the way to somewhere else.[7] In such a conception, judgment as a decisive moment separating the entirety of our mortal journey from the eternity of our reward makes perfect sense. If the journey is over, the destination can only be permanent, fixed. Even the fictional demon Michael sees the problem there: "But . . . these four humans got better after they died. That's not supposed to be possible. . . . The system by which we judge humans, the very method we use to deem them good or bad is so fundamentally flawed and unreasonable that hundreds of millions of people have been wrongly condemned to an eternity of torture."[8]

Latter-day Saints are in Michael's camp because they begin with a different conception of mortality. True enough, this is "a time to prepare," says Alma (12:24), and we are to be "proved herewith," relates Abraham (3:25). But what does it mean to be proved? In the era in which Joseph wrote those words, the term *proved* meant "to ascertain *some unknown quality* . . . by an experiment." "To experience . . . to gain certain knowledge by the operation of something on ourselves."[9] We are not taking a test—we are undergoing a process. Eternity is long, and we are in its morning. If progress is eternal and ongoing, then all humankind continues on a journey (*homo viator*) for a long time to come. This is the view of poet Christian Wiman:

> "All Creation groaneth and travaileth in pain together," says Paul, which is exactly right. But also this: all creation, including every atom of our selves, groaneth and travaileth toward something—not toward some ideal existence from which "sin" has irretrievably separated us, and not toward some heaven that is simply this existence times eternity. No. Faith is not faith in some state beyond change. Faith is faith *in* change.[10]

That is a marvelous, distinctive feature of Latter-day Saint thought, the implications of which we tend to forget in contemplating final judgment. When we give a "final" exam to students, it is not the last one they ever take. It marks the completion of a phase, one stage in ongoing education. The exam is an assessment, a point of clarification and transition between what has been learned and what remains to be learned or mastered. Some of the language of the Book of Mormon suggests that judgment in the eternal plan fulfills a comparable function. Alma's language describing Judgment Day is instructive: "This death, of which I have spoken, which is the temporal, shall deliver up its dead; which death is the grave. . . . And all men become incorruptible, and immortal, and they are living souls, having a perfect knowledge like unto us in the flesh, save it be that our knowledge shall be perfect." What is this "perfect knowledge" of which he speaks? It is not a divine omniscience; rather, it is a thoroughgoing self-awareness: "Wherefore, we shall have a perfect knowledge of all our guilt, and our uncleanness, and our nakedness; and the righteous shall have a perfect knowledge of their enjoyment, and their righteousness, being clothed with purity, yea, even with the robe of righteousness" (2 Ne. 9:11–14).

Such a perfect knowledge of our guilt hardly sounds like the gift of a benevolent God, if it is for the purpose of intensifying our suffering through the eternities. Most of us are quite capable of wallowing in our guilt without more provocation from the outside. But if this judgment, this self-illumination and self-understanding, is a prelude to further progress, it is a gift. Painful it may be in some cases, to confront ourselves in a moral mirror. But to have a "perfect knowledge of our enjoyment" suggests that we will also have revealed to us the grounds for a healthier and happier appreciation of what we accomplished in a terror-strewn landscape of death and suffering traversed in all-too-human weakness. Marilynne Robinson may be close to the mark in this regard: "In eternity this world will be Troy, I believe, and all that has passed here will be the epic of the universe, the ballad they sing in the streets."[11]

Dame Julian learned in her vision of judgment to see her own sins, so-called, through divine eyes that are both compassion-ate and understanding: "Here I saw verily that it was reluctance and frailty of the flesh without assent of the soul, for which God assigns no blame."[12] If this is a truer version of what the Day of Judgment portends, then we can understand why Elder Uchtdorf would refer to that day as a "day of mercy and love—a day when broken hearts are healed, when tears of grief are replaced with tears of gratitude, when all will be made right."[13] As the prescient Julian observes, "He desires that we have this confidence, that we be as secure in the hope of the bliss of heaven while we are here as we shall have the certainty when we are there."[14]

The First Vision is generally heralded as the opening of the dispensation in which all things are renewed. What is the greatest lesson we can take from young Joseph's experience? Let us propose something quite simple and elemental and infinitely transformative. Joseph said he was motivated to turn to God for guidance by reading a passage in James: "If any of you lack wisdom, let him ask of God, that giveth to all men liberally, and upbraideth not; and it shall be given him" (James 1:5). In another place and time, Enos was brought to his knees by remembering his father's words about "eternal life" and "the joy of the Saints" (Enos 1:3). He was enticed by God's love, not driven by fear of God's wrath. Joseph, however, inherited a different world, as his words reveal. He did not set off immediately for the grove. He hints how his reservations were overcome, in language that is highly suggestive of what had held him back. It was only after long consideration that God might "not upbraid" him that he decided he "might venture." In the language of that day, Joseph hoped that God might not "reprove [him] with severity," or "reproach [him]." And that he might, with confidence, "risk . . . danger."[15]

Joseph's initial trepidation to seek God calls to mind a pattern that goes back centuries. Martin Luther, his biographer writes, had a "crushing sense of worthlessness and fear of damnation."[16] He felt "a righteous God's fury against his sin," writes another historian.[17] The founder of Methodism, John Wesley, and thousands of his contemporaries, were driven to prayer by fear, anxiety and guilt. Joseph found scriptural basis for a more hopeful approach to deity. And what was the greatest truth that Joseph learned from his encounter in the Sacred Grove? Perhaps it wasn't anything about God's form, the state of the world, or what church to join. Here are the Lord's own words: "Joseph, my son, thy sins are forgiven thee. Go thy way, walk in my statutes, and keep my commandments. Behold, I am the Lord of glory. I was crucified for the world, that all those who believe on my name may have eternal life." And Joseph's response? "My soul was filled with love, and for many days I could rejoice with great joy."[18] Joseph had rediscovered the God of absolute love—a God who waits to embrace, not to condemn.

Life is hard, and demanding, and perilous. No one knows this more than He who experienced all our pain and all our sorrow. Joseph said the absolute precondition for a faith capable of exalting the human family is a correct knowledge of God's attributes. That spring morning, Joseph learned the most important of God's attributes. As Joseph would later teach, God is "merciful, and gracious, slow to anger, long suffering, and full of goodness. . . . Those who know their weakness and liability to sin, would be in constant doubt of salvation, if it were not for the idea which they have of the . . . character of God. . . . An idea of these facts does away with doubt, and makes faith exceeding strong."[19] In simpler language, the Lord Himself tried to assuage the myriad doubts He knew would afflict us all: "I came not to judge the world, but to heal the world" (John 12:47).[20]

To the extent that judgment plays a role in our future lives, Eugene England captured its Restoration import: "Judgment will be simply our complete self-knowledge and our consequent acceptance of the best opportunities and environment for further progress that we are able and willing to accept from a perfectly loving God."[21] An eighteenth-century Christian,

John "Salvation" Murray, described what happened when he started viewing God not as a God of wrath and judgment but as a God whose love was universal: "I regarded my friends with increasing affection, and I conceived, if I had an opportunity of conversing with the whole world, the whole world would be convinced." Murray's wife shared the renewed outlook: "When I contrast my days of ignorance with those on which the Sun of Righteousness hath dawned, I am wrapt in pleasure."[22]

NOTES

1 *Catholic Encyclopedia*, s.v., "Particular Judgment," accessed July 10, 2020, http://www.newadvent.org/cathen/08550a.htm.

2 John Calvin, *Sermons on Genesis: Chapters 1–11*, trans. Rob Roy McGregor (Edinburgh: The Banner of Truth, 2009), 259.

3 *The Good Place*, season 2, episode 13, "Somewhere Else," written and directed by Michael Schur, aired February 1, 2018 on NBC.

4 Anon., "Do What Is Right," in *The Psalms of Life* (Boston, 1857), in *Hymns* (Salt Lake City: The Church of Jesus Christ of Latter-day Saints, 1985), no. 237.

5 Ignatius, cited in Marcellino D'Ambrosio, *Who Were the Church Fathers?* (London: SPCK, 2015), 25.

6 Diarmaid MacCulloch, *Thomas Cranmer: A Life* (New Haven: Yale University Press, 1996), 510, 506.

7 Josef Pieper, *Death and Immortality* (South Bend, IN: St. Augustine's Press, 2000), 75–76.

8 *The Good Place*, "Somewhere Else."

9 *Noah Webster's First Edition of an American Dictionary of the English Language* (New York: S. Converse, 1828; repr. San Francisco: Foundation for American Christian Education, 1995), s.v. "prove."

10 Christian Wiman, *My Bright Abyss* (New York: Farrar, Straus and Giroux, 2014), 104.

11 Marilynne Robinson, *Gilead* (New York: Picador, 2004), 57.

12 Denise N. Baker, ed., *The Showings of Julian of Norwich*, 8.19 (New York: Norton, 2005), 31. We have modernized the spelling and at times modified the translation.

13 Dieter F. Uchtdorf, "O How Great the Plan of Our God!," *Ensign* 46, no. 11 (November 2016), 21.

14 Baker, *Showings of Julian of Norwich*, 15.65, p. 101.

15 *Webster's First Edition*, s.v. "upbraid," "venture."

16 Michael Massing, *Fatal Discord: Erasmus, Luther, and the Fight for the Western Mind* (New York: HarperCollins, 2018), 117.

17 Diarmaid MacCulloch, *The Reformation: A History* (New York: Viking, 2004), 116.

18 "History, circa Summer 1832," in *The Joseph Smith Papers: Histories, vol. 1, 1832–1844* (Salt Lake City, UT: Church Historian's Press, 2012), 5.

19 Theology Lecture Third, 1835 D&C, p. 39.

20 The critical term in this verse, once again, is *sodzo*, which we here render as "heal."

21 Eugene England, "Becoming a World Religion: Blacks, the Poor— All of Us," *Sunstone* 21, no. 2 (June–July 1998): 49–60.

22 Kathryn Gin Lum, *Damned Nation: Hell in American from the Revolution to Reconstruction* (New York: Oxford University Press, 2014), 21, 27.

PART THREE

Reframing the
Narrative

CHAPTER SEVENTEEN

Apostasy

From Total Eclipse to Wilderness Refuge

I n articulating the Restoration's relationship to other faith traditions, careful and charitable navigation is essential. Twin imperatives impel us in two directions, but in both directions danger lurks, a Scylla and a Charybdis each inviting disaster. One imperative is to recognize the essential goodness—*and inspired insights*—of those across the faith spectrum. As Brigham Young preached, men "naturally love and admire righteousness, justice and truth more than they do evil."[1] Goodness and inspiration transcend all categories and faith traditions. The other imperative is to clarify what developments in doctrine, and what abandoned "plain and precious things," account for the "awful woundedness" Nephi referenced, and which necessitated the Restoration. The twin dangers are, on the one hand, to ignore the vast array of God-touched figures across time and culture who contributed their share of light and truth, and, on the other, to downplay—in the interest of interfaith bridge-building—very real corruptions and changes to such an extent that we render the Restoration superfluous at worst or a mild corrective at best.

In other words, charity and humility require that we actively seek to discover and celebrate truth *wherever* we find it in the Christian past and present. "Receive truth let it come from where it may," was Mormonism's "grand fundamental principle,"

Joseph said.[2] And commitment to the value of the Restoration requires that we actively seek to clarify and fully appreciate the distinctive work of repair and reform that the Restoration was intended to accomplish. These twin sensibilities were commended by Peter when he directed disciples in how they should defend their faith. Be ready to explain the reason for the hope that is in you, he said, "with meekness and a wholesome serious caution" (1 Pet. 3:15; Wuest trans.).

One principle that is helpful in this regard is articulated by Diana Bass. She notes that in narrating the Christian past, "the usual story is that of 'Big-C' Christianity—Christ, Constantine, Christendom, Calvin, and Christian America."[3] And, we would add, Creeds and Crusades. There is much to lament and even to condemn in this history, as Bass readily acknowledges. However, her point is that Big-C Christianity is not the important entity, and creeds are not what define Christian practice or the character of Christian believers. She invokes a principle—*sensus fidelium*—or the "natural wisdom" of the faithful—to contrast official dogma with real-world belief. A historian of the Reformation concurs: "Religion as practiced even by the self-consciously orthodox was not necessarily the same as religion that was officially recommended."[4]

Our experience has borne this out: one is hard-pressed to find an average Baptist who has even read the Westminster Confession, an Anglican who knows the content of the Thirty-nine Articles, or a lay Catholic who knows the difference between *homoousios* and *homoiousios*[5]—though conformity to those formulae and distinctions were matters of life and death at various times in the Christian past. As a Methodist theologian once told us, in explaining his personal divergence from one stipulated dogma, "We don't really pay much attention to the creeds."

On the other hand, one can live in blithe indifference to, or in ignorance of, one's historical foundations and still be profoundly shaped by them in ways large and small. That conviction underlies this book's central thesis: belief shapes culture, which shapes language, which continues to shape culture. (The actual process is messier and nonlinear, but that's the main point.) So, in tracing some key moments and features in Christian thought, we were not creating a straw man: our purpose has been to emphasize key doctrines that were spiritually and morally catastrophic—doctrines that, regardless of their lesser modern authority among a plurality of Christians, held great sway at one time and linger on in their subtle influence today. Neither is an appraisal of creedal formulations an indictment of any believers then or now. The Lord Himself referred to Christian creeds as "an abomination," and yet the Book of Mormon explicitly absolves the generality of "gentiles" from blame for their "woundedness" and "blindness" that results from the loss of the gospel's "plain and most precious parts" (1 Ne. 13:32). In fact, and this takes us to our next point, the Lord made clear to Joseph Smith that beauty and truth persisted through the centuries that intervened between the Crucifixion and the First Vision. And that pattern, which Joseph came to recognize, gave definition to what we may have poorly understood by the words *Apostasy*, *Restoration*, and *Church*.

Joseph Smith seems to have come gradually to his understanding of the task—and meaning—of the Restoration. One glimpse into his mind may be found in a revision to a revelation he produced in 1833. The backstory begins, however, in 1795. That was the year the Scottish minister Alexander Fraser published his popular work *Key to the Prophecies*, which included an interpretation of a passage from the twelfth chapter of the book of Revelation. This was a chapter of immense interest to Protestants because it was read by them—and would also be read by Joseph Smith—as a prophecy of what they were calling the Great Apostasy. The chapter relates how a woman is confronted by a dragon (who led one-third of the stars of heaven to fall). Under this threat, the woman "fled into the wilderness." Adam Clark, the commentator upon whom Joseph most relied, identified the woman described in that chapter's allegory as the Christian Church, as did most Protestant writers. And so we have, in brief, the history of the original Christian church, which is threatened by Satan and consequently disappears. The Apostasy, in other words.

Fraser, however, saw a silver lining in his reading of Revelation chapter 12. For the church in the wilderness, according to the words of prophecy, is "fed by the word and Spirit of God" ("nourished for a time," in John's words). This nourishment took place, Fraser wrote, "without the outward ordinances, . . . which . . . were defiled," it is true. But otherwise, in Fraser's vision, the "true church of Christ" is rendered invisible, protected, nourished, and preserved during these centuries.[6] Here we find a significantly different understanding of Christian history than the one long dominant in Latter-day Saint culture. Rather than the total loss of truth, the absence of all light and inspiration, we find in Fraser's reading a story of survival—underground, at the margins, "in the wilderness." What a marvelously expansive, wonderfully open-ended story this reading presents us with! We have here a vision of a dispersed community of the honest in heart: nurtured, fed, inspired, and instructed by the Spirit during their long sojourn in the wilderness.

Evidence suggests that Joseph Smith was inspired by Fraser's reading. Between 1833 and 1835, Joseph modified the language of a revelation to mirror Fraser's point. In 1833, in a first reference to giving the Restoration institutional form, a revelation referred to Joseph's assignment to "work a reformation" and "establish [the Lord's] church" (Book of Commandments 4:5). While that language was not terribly specific, it did suggest modifying an existing set of beliefs (*reformation*) while building something new (*establish*). Two years later, however, Joseph significantly reframed this revelation, giving to the principle of Restoration a very different modus operandi and purpose. He did so under the apparent inspiration of Fraser's prophecy and even his language. Fraser had anticipated the future day when, after its exile in the wilderness, "the universal church shall again become visible as a community, extended over the whole earth, 'clear as the sun, fair as the moon, and terrible as an army with banners,'" borrowing that imagery from Song of Solomon (6:10).[7]

In reworking the revelation for the 1835 Doctrine and Covenants, Joseph confirmed Fraser's point—that the Church would emerge from a wilderness exile—and used Fraser's precise language from the Song of Solomon. The promised day had come, Joseph declared, and we were now "in this the beginning of the rising up and the coming forth of my church out of the wilderness—clear as the moon, and fair as the sun, and terrible as an army with banners" (now D&C 5:14). The work of Restoration would require a gathering—but more than scattered Israel would need to be reassembled.

NOTES

1   Richard S. Van Wagoner, ed., *Complete Discourses of Brigham Young* (Salt Lake City: Smith-Petit Foundation, 2009), 4:2020.

2   Andrew F. Ehat and Lyndon W. Cook, *The Words of Joseph Smith* (Orem, UT: Grandin Book Company, 1991), 229.

3   Diana Butler Bass, *A People's History of Christianity* (New York: HarperCollins, 1989), 4.

4   Diarmaid MacCulloch, *The Reformation: A History* (New York: Viking, 2004), 15.

5   *Homoousios* and *homoiousios*, "of the same" and "of a similar substance," respectively, differentiated contending factions arguing in the fourth century over the relationship of the Father and the Son.

6   Alexander Fraser, *Key to the Prophecies of the Old and New Testaments, which are not yet accomplished* (Philadelphia: John Bioren, 1802 [1795]), 157–159.

7   Fraser, *Key to the Prophecies*, 164.

CHAPTER EIGHTEEN

Restoration

From Ex Nihilo to Out of the Wilderness

So what is the significance of this shift in language, from a church that is newly "established" to one that is shepherded back from the wilderness? To say that one will bring something out of exile—be it a scattered Israel or the Lord's Church—is simultaneously to say two things. First, that the entity was never entirely lost in the first place, only dispersed and broken. And second, that the process of Restoration means to gather, assemble, and recontextualize gospel truths in light of that original master blueprint. Joseph quickly came to recognize that, like the ruins of an ancient temple, beautiful remnants of the original Church lay all about them, "broken . . . rent, and disjointed," as "scattered fragments of Mormonism."[1] Thereafter, when Joseph found these scattered fragments, whether he found them in the philosopher Thomas Dick, the commentator Adam Clark, or the Universalist theologian John Taylor, he placed them into the larger framework of Restoration teachings.[2] And he taught the Saints to do likewise: "If the Presbyterians have any truth, embrace that. If the Baptists and Methodists have truth, embrace that too. Get all the good in the world if you want to come out a pure Mormon."[3]

Suddenly, we are all tasked—and empowered—with re-discovering the lost treasures of our Christian heritage that were sidelined, ignored, or often explicitly condemned. The more we look appreciatively upon the past, the more we discover that virtually every element of the Great Story, the Plan of Happiness, survived in some corner of the world, in some neglected treatise or mystic's visionary work, a preacher's homilies or the insights of a "heretic." Our premortal lives were affirmed by the ancient Origen and the young Augustine. They were written about beautifully and prolifically by the pure-souled Thomas Traherne ("How like an angel came I down!"),[4] and were stoutly defended (at the cost of his career) by the little-known but deeply inspired Edward Beecher.[5] Mortality as a planned ascent into the educative crucible of "trial by existence" was clearly taught by the second-century church father Irenaeus (God organized all things from the beginning for "the bringing of man to perfection, for his edification, . . . that man might finally be brought to maturity at some future time").[6]

As Joseph would, John Wesley taught that heaven was to consist largely of the sociability that we foster here in community, which was "the grand reason why God is pleased to assist men by men, rather than immediately by himself, . . . to endear us to each other by these mutual good offices, in order to increase our happiness both in time and eternity."[7] God's ultimate designs for the human family, taught Origen, are to "impart deification to others . . . who are transformed through him into gods, as images of the prototype."[8]

Regarding those not fortunate enough to embrace the gospel here, Origen understood spirit prison and the evangelization of the dead almost two millennia before Joseph F. Smith's recovery of that truth. Origin wrote, "I think . . . that all the saints who depart from this life will remain in some place situated on the earth which holy Scripture calls paradise, as in some place of instruction and, so to speak, class-room or school of souls.'"[9]

Tertullian broke with the early Church when he chose to defend belief in the continuation of gifts of prophecy and revelation; George MacDonald had no patience with the constraints of narrow orthodoxy implied by a closed canon: "A thousand questions will arise to which the Bible does not even allude. . . . Sad, indeed, would the whole matter be, if the Bible told us everything God meant us to believe."[10] What a remarkable endorsement of continuing revelation.

As a people, we have just begun to sift the Christian past for survivals of the original deposit of faith. *Not* to corroborate or defend our claims, but to enrich, expand, and shape our own devotion and knowledge. Many Church members have imagined the so-called Apostasy to be a time of total darkness, total absence of God's light and truth from the earth. It would be more generous to our fellow Christians, as well as more accurate to Joseph Smith's understanding, to see that term as the loss of the story's essential plot. Originally, the narrative went like this:

> Our lives are traceable to a premortal sphere in which God the Eternal Father and God the Eternal Mother invited us, spirit beings, into eternal relationship with Themselves. Rather than creating humans for Their own glory, God chose to nurture these souls along a path of mortal education so that all women and men "might have joy." It is at this moment, before the earth is created or the first person formed, that grace—God's freely given offering of love—irrupts into the universe. On the one hand, this grace is manifest in God's vulnerable exposure as nurturing Parents, co-suffering in Their children's travails and pains along their way to exaltation. On the other, this grace is manifest in that willingness of the Only Begotten, Jesus Christ, to consecrate His life, His death, and His still-continuing efforts to heal us, nurture us, and bring us home. With these gracious resources, and by our deliberate choice, we embarked upon a course of guided transformation into holier beings committed to building holy community (Zion). As our hearts are educated

and tutored by the Holy Spirit, we bring ourselves into conformity with the divine nature and anticipate a reunion as part of a heavenly, eternal family.

The main features of that story evaporate under the influence of Augustine, and new, alien narratives are established by Luther and Calvin. Apostasy might best be characterized as the loss of that framing context in light of which the various characters and themes in the story fit together and make sense. As for Restoration—as a people we have tended to see a process of simple replacement of error with truth. A preferable reading would be to understand Restoration as beginning with the recuperation of that original "everlasting covenant" established in premortal worlds, which endows our lives with their true origin, purpose, and destiny as children of Heavenly Parents. The ongoing work of Restoration consists in the continued work of searching out, celebrating, and recontextualizing treasures "new and old" (Matt. 13:52). In the economy of heaven, we do not need to sow and reap where some of the crop already lies abroad in the land, long ready to harvest.

NOTES

1   "The Religion of the Ancients," *Times and Seasons* 4, no. 9 (March 15, 1843):136; Not the Prophet, S.T.P., "To the Editor," *Times and Seasons* 5, no. 8 (April 15, 1844): 503.

2   Sometimes Smith acknowledged the source, as he did with Dick. Other times, he seems to have simply adopted perspectives and examples he found to be inspired. For example, anticipating Doctrine and Covenants 19, Murray reasoned that the pain of a candle flame is brief, but the pain is still "of everlasting fire." John Murray, *Letters and Sketches of Sermons* (Boston: Joshua Belcher, 1812), 2:253.

3   Andrew F. Ehat and Lyndon W. Cook, *The Words of Joseph Smith* (Orem, UT: Grandin Book Company, 1991), 234.

4   Thomas Traherne, "Wonder," in *Selected Writings of Thomas Traherne*, ed. Dick Davis (Manchester: Fyfield, 1980), 20.

5   See especially Edward Beecher, *The Conflict of Ages: or, the Great Debate on the Moral Relations of God and Man* (Boston: Phillips, Sampson, 1853).

6   Irenaeus, *Against Heresies*, 4.37.7, in *The Ante-Nicene Fathers* [hereafter *ANF*], ed. Alexander Roberts and James Donaldson, (Grand Rapids: Eerdmans, 1977), 1:520–21.

7   John Wesley, "Of Good Angels," in *Sermons on Several Occasions* (Nashville: E. Stevenson & F. A. Owen, 1855), 3:206.

8   Origen, "Man," in *The Early Christian Fathers*, ed. and trans. Henry Bettenson (Oxford: Oxford University Press, 1969), 274.

9   Origen, *First Principles* 2.11.6, *ANF* 4:299.

10   George Macdonald, "The Higher Faith," in *Unspoken Sermons*, 1st ser. (Whitehorn, CA: Johannesen, 2004), 35–37.

CHAPTER NINETEEN

Church

From Reservoir of the Righteous to Collaborators with Christ

A nd what, then, of the Church? Irenaeus, before darkness overtook the Christian understanding of God, referred to Christianity as "the only true and life-giving faith."[1] Perhaps that is a more accurate rendering of our own phrase, "true and living," because it emphasizes what our faith—if accurately articulated—is capable of *doing*. In an important sense, scripture—including modern scripture—refers to the Church in two distinct, equally important ways. We have the *institutional Church*, with its formal incorporation and programs and policies and buildings. Its role is essential and indispensable, both for channeling the powers of heaven through temple ordinances and for creating the optimum environment in which we may learn the hard task of indiscriminate love.

In addition to this meaning, Joseph's predecessors and contemporaries believed the church in the wilderness symbolized the reality of an *invisible Church*, where righteous individuals, their spiritual gifts, and godly principles and practices persisted. It is striking that in Joseph Smith's revelations, we find recurrent hints, intimations, and outright directives to remember that the institutional Church is not the exhaustive repository of the chosen or the blessed. We would do well to think of the Church, with its temples and priesthood, as the universal portal to the

Heavenly Family, not as the reservoir of the righteous. While the institutional Church has an important role in the Lord's eternal purposes (primarily the stewardship of the temple and its sealing ordinances), we might profitably keep this other version of His Church in mind. If this Church, like Zion, consists of "the pure in heart," then we need to be looking beyond traditional boundaries to encounter our fellow Saints.

One of the clearest confirmations of Joseph's understanding of a holy Church in the wilderness came by revelation in May 1831, when the Lord revealed that in the background, independent of the Latter-day Saint Restoration, God had reserved unto himself "holy men," about whom Joseph knew nothing (D&C 49:8). An 1829 revelation—a year *before* the Restoration—also referred to Christ's Church as already existing, and the Lord spoke words of comfort to its members ("whosoever belongeth to my church need not fear, for such shall inherit the kingdom of heaven" [D&C 10:55]). The Lord reassures those faithful that "*this part of my gospel*" about to come forth will be a boon to them: "I do not bring [this part of my gospel] to destroy that which they have received . . . and again . . . I do not say this to destroy my church, but I say this to build up my church; Therefore, whosoever belongeth to my church need not fear, for such shall inherit the kingdom of heaven" (D&C 10:51–55).

To which church is God, therefore, referring, if the restored Church had not yet been formed? The Book of Mormon refers to a Church of the Lamb of God, that apparently transcends any particular historical moment or incarnation. Nephi defines *covenant identity* as those who will have "the Lord" to be their God (1 Ne. 17:40). In that ancient American record, covenant identity begins as a family grouping—and the Nephites were particularly concerned about the survival of their line—but by the time of Christ's coming, Nephites are a group defined by their faith, not their ancestry. Through numerous dislocations and places of settlement (and promised lands) the Nephites learn that Zion is a portable, figurative tent in the wilderness. All these precedents comprise a prescient warning against the tendency to associate Zion with a particular place, people, nationality, religion, or historical moment.

B. H. Roberts saw and understood the radical significance of that 1829 revelation. "From this it very clearly appears that the purpose of God in the introduction of the Dispensation of the Fulness of Times was not to destroy any truth that existed in the world, but to add to that truth, to increase it, and to draw together all truth and develop it into a beautiful system in which men may rest contented, knowing God and their relationship to him, knowing of the future and their relation to that future."[2] Was this what Paul saw prophetically, as that future day when God "might gather together in one *all* things in Christ"? (Eph. 1:10). That "God may be all in all"? (1 Cor. 15:28).

We need to find new ways of balancing faith in the divine foundations and mission of the restored Church, with a humility of language and self-conception, a generosity of vision, appropriate to its destiny. Jacob Boehme referred to this invisible Church as the "church without walls."[3] Martin Luther King Jr. appealed to the "tireless efforts of men [and women] willing to be co-workers with God."[4] William Penn calls the Zion builders "the humble, meek, merciful, just, pious, and devout souls who are everywhere of one religion; and when death has taken off the mask, they will know one another, though the diverse liveries they wear here make them strangers."[5] Elder Theodore M. Burton warned Latter-day Saints that we have a tendency to forget that "we are part of a total community . . . that we are all members of one family, for God hath made of one blood all nations (Acts 17:26)."[6]

As the gospel settles into an increasing number of cultural environments, the kingdom will continue to unfold as a beautiful tapestry of many threads, if we do not hinder its progress. Zion will continue to be found, and to be built up, in an array of settings. And like the wind that bloweth where it listeth, with its invisible comings and goings, the Church of the Lamb of God will reach farther than we can possibly know:

> And then shall none of us be stirred up to say . . . "Lord, if it had only been thus, it had been well." But we shall all say with one voice, "Lord, blessed must thou be, for it is thus, it *is* well."[7]

NOTES

1   Irenaeus, *Against Heresies*, 3, preface in *The Ante-Nicene Fathers*, ed. Alexander Roberts and James Donaldson (Grand Rapids: Eerdmans, 1977), 1:414.

2   B. H. Roberts. "The Relationship of the Church to the Christian Sects: The Doctrine of Two Churches Only" in *Defense of the Faith and the Saints* (Salt Lake City: Deseret News, 1907), 1:31, 34–36.

3   "Die Kirche ohne mauer," letter 46 in *Jacob Boehme*, ed. Robin Waterfield (Berkeley: North Atlantic Books, 2001), 16.

4   Martin Luther King, *Why We Can't Wait* (New York: Signet Classic, 2000), 74. Quoted in Patrick Q. Mason, *Planted: Belief and Belonging in an Age of Doubt* (Salt Lake City: Deseret Book; Provo: Neal A. Maxwell Institute, 2015), 112.

5   William Penn, "Some Fruits of Solitude," in *Harvard Classics: Franklin, Woolman, Penn* (New York: Collier and Son, 1969), 364.

6   Theodore M. Burton, "Blessed Are the Peacemakers," *Ensign* 4, no. 11 (November 1974): 54.

7   Denise N. Baker, ed., *The Showings of Julian of Norwich*, 85 (New York: Norton, 2005), 124.

Index